OPPOSING VIEWPOINTS® SERIES

Genocide

Other Books of Related Interest

Opposing Viewpoints Series

Human Migration
Human Trafficking
Peoples on the Move: The Immigration Crisis

At Issue Series

Genocide
Open Borders
Reproductive Rights

Current Controversies Series

Hate Groups
Nativism, Nationalism, and Patriotism
Reparations for Black Americans

> "Congress shall make no law … abridging the freedom of speech, or of the press."
>
> *First Amendment to the U.S. Constitution*

The basic foundation of our democracy is the First Amendment guarantee of freedom of expression. The Opposing Viewpoints series is dedicated to the concept of this basic freedom and the idea that it is more important to practice it than to enshrine it.

OPPOSING VIEWPOINTS® SERIES

Genocide

Lisa Idzikowski, Book Editor

GREENHAVEN PUBLISHING

Published in 2023 by Greenhaven Publishing, LLC
2544 Clinton Street,
Buffalo NY 14224

First Edition

Articles in Greenhaven Publishing anthologies are often edited for length to meet page requirements. In addition, original titles of these works are changed to clearly present the main thesis and to explicitly indicate the author's opinion. Every effort is made to ensure that Greenhaven Publishing accurately reflects the original intent of the authors. Every effort has been made to trace the owners of the copyrighted material.

Cover image: Olexiy Kryvych/Shutterstock.com

Library of Congress CataloginginPublication Data

Names: Idzikowski, Lisa, editor.
Title: Genocide / edited by Lisa Idzikowski.
Description: First Edition. | New York : Greenhaven Publishing, 2024. | Series: Opposing viewpoints | Includes bibliographic references and index.
Identifiers: ISBN 9781534509313 (pbk.) | ISBN 9781534509320 (library bound)
Subjects: LCSH: Genocide--Juvenile literature.
Classification: LCC HV6322.7 G445 2024 | DDC 364.15'1--dc23

Manufactured in the United States of America

Website: http://greenhavenpublishing.com

Contents

The Importance of Opposing Viewpoints

Perhaps every generation experiences a period in time in which the populace seems especially polarized, starkly divided on the important issues of the day and gravitating toward the far ends of the political spectrum and away from a consensus-facilitating middle ground. The world that today's students are growing up in and that they will soon enter into as active and engaged citizens is deeply fragmented in just this way. Issues relating to terrorism, immigration, women's rights, minority rights, race relations, health care, taxation, wealth and poverty, the environment, policing, military intervention, the proper role of government—in some ways, perennial issues that are freshly and uniquely urgent and vital with each new generation—are currently roiling the world.

If we are to foster a knowledgeable, responsible, active, and engaged citizenry among today's youth, we must provide them with the intellectual, interpretive, and critical-thinking tools and experience necessary to make sense of the world around them and of the all-important debates and arguments that inform it. After all, the outcome of these debates will in large measure determine the future course, prospects, and outcomes of the world and its peoples, particularly its youth. If they are to become successful members of society and productive and informed citizens, students need to learn how to evaluate the strengths and weaknesses of someone else's arguments, how to sift fact from opinion and fallacy, and how to test the relative merits and validity of their own opinions against the known facts and the best possible available information. The landmark series Opposing Viewpoints has been providing students with just such critical-thinking skills and exposure to the debates surrounding society's most urgent contemporary issues for many years, and it continues to serve this essential role with undiminished commitment, care, and rigor.

The key to the series's success in achieving its goal of sharpening students' critical-thinking and analytic skills resides in its title—

Opposing Viewpoints. In every intriguing, compelling, and engaging volume of this series, readers are presented with the widest possible spectrum of distinct viewpoints, expert opinions, and informed argumentation and commentary, supplied by some of today's leading academics, thinkers, analysts, politicians, policy makers, economists, activists, change agents, and advocates. Every opinion and argument anthologized here is presented objectively and accorded respect. There is no editorializing in any introductory text or in the arrangement and order of the pieces. No piece is included as a "straw man," an easy ideological target for cheap point-scoring. As wide and inclusive a range of viewpoints as possible is offered, with no privileging of one particular political ideology or cultural perspective over another. It is left to each individual reader to evaluate the relative merits of each argument—as he or she sees it, and with the use of ever-growing critical-thinking skills—and grapple with his or her own assumptions, beliefs, and perspectives to determine how convincing or successful any given argument is and how the reader's own stance on the issue may be modified or altered in response to it.

This process is facilitated and supported by volume, chapter, and selection introductions that provide readers with the essential context they need to begin engaging with the spotlighted issues, with the debates surrounding them, and with their own perhaps shifting or nascent opinions on them. In addition, guided reading and discussion questions encourage readers to determine the authors' point of view and purpose, interrogate and analyze the various arguments and their rhetoric and structure, evaluate the arguments' strengths and weaknesses, test their claims against available facts and evidence, judge the validity of the reasoning, and bring into clearer, sharper focus the reader's own beliefs and conclusions and how they may differ from or align with those in the collection or those of their classmates.

Research has shown that reading comprehension skills improve dramatically when students are provided with compelling, intriguing, and relevant "discussable" texts. The subject matter of these collections could not be more compelling, intriguing, or urgently relevant to today's students and the world they are poised to inherit. The anthologized articles and the reading and discussion questions that are included with them also provide the basis for stimulating, lively, and passionate classroom debates. Students who are compelled to anticipate objections to their own argument and identify the flaws in those of an opponent read more carefully, think more critically, and steep themselves in relevant context, facts, and information more thoroughly. In short, using discussable text of the kind provided by every single volume in the Opposing Viewpoints series encourages close reading, facilitates reading comprehension, fosters research, strengthens critical thinking, and greatly enlivens and energizes classroom discussion and participation. The entire learning process is deepened, extended, and strengthened.

For all of these reasons, Opposing Viewpoints continues to be exactly the right resource at exactly the right time—when we most need to provide readers with the critical-thinking tools and skills that will not only serve them well in school but also in their careers and their daily lives as decision-making family members, community members, and citizens. This series encourages respectful engagement with and analysis of opposing viewpoints and fosters a resulting increase in the strength and rigor of one's own opinions and stances. As such, it helps make readers "future ready," and that readiness will pay rich dividends for the readers themselves, for the citizenry, for our society, and for the world at large.

Introduction

> *"Genocide is not just a murderous madness; it is, more deeply, a politics that promises a utopia beyond politics—one people, one land, one truth, the end of difference. Since genocide is a form of political utopia, it remains an enduring temptation in any multiethnic and multicultural society in crisis."*
>
> *-Michael Ignatieff, Canadian author, academic, and former politician*

The act of genocide is not a recent occurrence. The Holocaust (1941–1945), perhaps the most familiar case of genocide, was perpetrated by Nazi Germany under Adolf Hitler during World War II. It was the first case of genocide since the term was coined in 1944 by Raphael Lemkin, although genocides had happened before that time and have continued into the present day. But as a result of the mass atrocities committed by Germany, the United Nations General Assembly approved an international agreement, the Convention on the Prevention and Punishment of the Crime of Genocide, on December 9, 1948. As of 2022, 152 member states (countries and other sovereign states) of the UN have signed on to this treaty.[1]

According to *Merriam-Webster,* the term genocide was first used in 1944, and is defined as "the deliberate and systematic destruction of a racial, political, or cultural group."[2] The United Nations, in its Genocide Convention, defines it "as a crime committed with the intent to destroy a national, ethnic, racial or religious group, in whole or in part."[3] The UN acknowledges that genocide has caused untold losses for humanity, and it has affected all people, including children of all ages and from all backgrounds in many different regions of the world.

In March of 2022, while at the Holocaust Memorial Museum in Washington, DC, U.S. Secretary of State, Antony Blinken said that "the day will come when those responsible for these appalling acts will have to answer for them."[4] Blinken made this remark during a talk about genocides happening around the world and what governments and individuals should do about it. Not surprisingly, according to a poll taken in October of 2022 by Reuters, 73 percent of Americans said that Washington should continue providing support for Ukraine in its conflict against Russia, which some people are already calling a genocide.[5] Another poll done by IPSOS in December of 2022 shows that almost half of Americans believed that the US should support Ukraine in its fight "for as long as it takes."[6]

According to the United States Holocaust Memorial Museum, there are a number of large scale crimes that are committed against populations of people. These include genocide, mass killing, ethnic cleansing, war crimes, and crimes against humanity.[7] What causes governments, leaders, military personnel, or ordinary citizens to go after a group of people or become complicit in mass violence? The reasons are complex and not easily understood. One factor seems to be a common thread. Dehumanization, or claiming that a certain group of people are "the other" and outside of one's own group is a tactic used by leaders wanting to incite genocidal violence. Another common tactic involves surrounding citizens with a flood of untruths and disinformation. Hitler did this to German citizens before the Holocaust began and Putin is doing this in Russia today.

These disturbing facts may be difficult to contemplate, but experts agree that there are avenues to lessening the chances of or to preventing genocide in the future. This volume examines important ideas about genocide. What is genocide? What part does dehumanization play in genocidal violence? Does genocide happen in democratic countries? Are the causes of brutality and violence always the same? And is there a way to prevent genocide in the future? Readers have the opportunity to contemplate and understand the timely questions surrounding the issue of genocide by reading *Opposing Viewpoints: Genocide*, which sheds light on this ongoing contemporary issue.

Notes

1. "The Genocide Convention," United Nations Office on Genocide Prevention and the Responsibility to Protect. https://www.un.org/en/genocideprevention/genocide-convention.shtml.
2. "Genocide," *Merriam-Webster*. https://www.merriam-webster.com/dictionary/genocide.
3. "Genocide, United Nations Office on Genocide Prevention and the Responsibility to Protect. https://www.un.org/en/genocideprevention/genocide.shtml.
4. Anthony Blinken, "Secretary Antony J. Blinken on the Genocide and Crimes Against Humanity in Burma, U.S. Department of State, March 21, 2022. https://www.state.gov/secretary-antony-j-blinken-at-the-united-states-holocaust-memorial-museum/.
5. Patricia Zengerle, "Three in four Americans say U.S. should support Ukraine despite Russian threats, Reuters/Ipsos poll shows," Reuters, October 5, 2022. https://www.reuters.com/world/europe/three-four-americans-say-us-should-support-ukraine-despite-russian-threats-2022-10-05/.
6. "Majority of American continue to support Ukraine, but have mixed views on war outlook," IPSOS, December 9, 2022. https://www.ipsos.com/sites/default/files/ct/news/documents/2022-12/Chicago%20Council%20Topline.pdf.
7. "Definitions: Types of Mass Atrocities," United States Holocaust Memorial Museum. https://www.ushmm.org/genocide-prevention/learn-about-genocide-and-other-mass-atrocities/definitions.

OPPOSING VIEWPOINTS® SERIES

Chapter 1

Is Genocide Different from War Crimes or Ethnic Cleansing?

Chapter Preface

What is genocide? Is it different from war crimes or ethnic cleansing? Some people may have a vague idea about the occurrence of genocide or war crimes or remember something about these issues from school. Others may be experiencing these situations firsthand, or through relatives or friends. In reality, genocide, war crimes, and ethnic cleansing have happened in the past, during times of war or peace, and are continuing to happen today.

The viewpoints in this chapter provide a solid foundation into the topic of genocide. Several authors analyze, outline, and define the concept itself while distinguishing genocide from war crimes or ethnic cleansing. Other viewpoints explain the fundamentals of international laws that attempt to both limit the occurrence of genocide or punish the perpetrators. Multiple viewpoints take a closer look at the UN Convention for the Prevention and Punishment of the Crime of Genocide from 1948, which laid the groundwork for defining and punishing genocide. An interesting addition to these ideas is that the authors offer suggestions for international community action to bolster these laws.

Other viewpoints in this chapter delve into genocides that are happening as of 2023 in Ukraine, have happened recently in Myanmar, or have happened in the past, particularly in relation to the Holocaust perpetrated by Nazi Germany. Through looking at these particular instances of genocide, it becomes possible to more clearly understand what the crime is. Readers will benefit from reading and thinking about the viewpoints in this chapter that provide a base of insight into the topic of genocide. By clarifying how the term "genocide" is commonly defined and distinguished from other similar but distinct crimes, it becomes possible to determine if an act does qualify as genocide and how best to address and punish it.

Viewpoint 1

> *"To qualify as genocide, the actions must be done with intent to eliminate an entire group of people. Without provable intent, a group or individual can still be guilty of 'crimes against humanity' or 'ethnic cleansing' but not genocide."*

The Difference Between Genocide and Ethnic Cleansing

Layla Quran

In the following viewpoint, Layla Quran analyzes and outlines exactly what constitutes a genocide. Quran contends that genocide and ethnic cleansing are not the same thing. She provides a clear explanation of the two events, along with examples of each type of event. Quran also explains why countries often are careful when defining atrocities committed against certain groups of people and why it is difficult to enforce international laws against genocide. Layla Quran previously was a foreign affairs producer and reporter for PBS. At the time this viewpoint was published, she was a general assignment producer for PBS NewsHour.

As you read, consider the following questions:

1. As stated in this viewpoint, what are the five acts of genocide?
2. What is the difference between genocide and ethnic cleansing, according to Quran?
3. How does the international community help support international law in cases of genocide, according to the author?

World leaders have chosen their words carefully when describing the mass exodus of Rohingya fleeing violence in Myanmar, so far largely avoiding the legally specific and politically charged term "genocide."

The actions the Myanmar military is taking against the Muslim minority group have been called a "complicated situation," a "brutal crackdown," and a "textbook case of ethnic cleansing."

On Tuesday, a U.S. state department official said the U.S. is considering new targeted sanctions against Myanmar but declined to label the violence ethnic cleaning.

Spokeswoman Heather Nauret said in a statement that the U.S. is restricting all assistance programs for those involved in the violence, halting travel waivers for senior Myanmar military leaders, and may use a human rights law to target specific groups or officials.

The Associated Press reports that U.S. officials are preparing a recommendation for Secretary of State Rex Tillerson to declare that ethnic cleansing is taking place in Myanmar, but the State Department declined to comment.

What Does 'Genocide' Technically Mean?

The United Nations first defined genocide in 1948 in the Convention on the Prevention and Punishment of the Crime of Genocide. The treaty outlines five acts that can constitute genocide if they

The Convention for the Prevention and Punishment of the Crime of Genocide

The Convention for the Prevention and Punishment of the Crime of Genocide was adopted by the United Nations General Assembly on 9 December 1948 and entered into force on 12 January 1951 when, in accordance with article 13, the twentieth instrument of ratification or accession was deposited at the United Nations.

According to the Convention, genocide means "any of the following acts committed with intent to destroy, in whole or in part, a national, ethnical, racial or religious group, as such: (a) Killing members of the group; (b) Causing serious bodily or mental harm to members of the group; (c) Deliberately inflicting on the group conditions of life calculated to bring about its physical destruction in whole or in part; (d) Imposing measures intended to prevent births within the group; (e) Forcibly transferring children of the group to another group.

"Convention on Genocide (1948)," Consejo Superior de Investigaciones Científicas (CSIC).

are done "with the intent to destroy an ethnic, national, racial or religious group":

1. Killing members of the group
2. Causing serious bodily or mental harm
3. Deliberately inflicting conditions of life calculated to bring about the group's physical destruction in whole or in part
4. Imposing measures intended to prevent births
5. Forcibly transferring children

To qualify as genocide, the actions must be done with intent to eliminate an entire group of people. Without provable intent, a group or individual can still be guilty of "crimes against humanity" or "ethnic cleansing" but not genocide.

Tribunals have historically struggled to establish a legal standard for genocidal intent. Few perpetrators, with the notable exception of the Nazi regime, have left explicit plans detailing their intentions to eradicate groups.

The first person found guilty of genocide was the former mayor of Rwanda's Taba commune in 1998. The International Genocide Tribunal on Rwanda found Jean-Paul Akayesu guilty because "he knew or should have known that the act committed would destroy, in whole or in part, a group."

What Is Ethnic Cleansing?

Ethnic cleansing, on the other hand, only refers to the expulsion of a group from a certain area.

Ethnic cleansing has not been defined and is not recognized as a crime under international law, according to the U.N. And in reality, the lines between ethnic cleansing and genocide are often blurred.

"Your motivation may be that you want the people out, but if in doing that you intend to destroy the group, then it's also genocide," said James Silk, a human rights professor at Yale Law School.

"International law lacks enforcement mechanisms, it demands buy in from an international community. Clearly it hasn't been effective."

More than 500,000 Rohingya refugees, escaping violence and persecution in Myanmar, have fled their homes in the last two months.

Rohingya refugees made their way across the border to Bangladesh in earlier spouts of violence in the 1970s and 1990s and again in October 2016. The latest wave of refugees occurred after Aug. 25, when Rohingya insurgents staged an attack on several police posts and an army base in the Rakhine state.

The Myanmar military retaliated against Rohingya villages in the Rakhine state, with accounts documenting villages burned, women and girls raped, and hundreds of Rohingya killed.

A U.N. report from September details the Myanmar government forces conducting a "well-coordinated, organized and systematic campaign of human rights violations" against the Rohingya ethnic minority, and the "forced displacement of large sections of the Rohingya population" from their villages.

What Is the Punishment for Genocide?

The U.N. treaty addressing genocide states that any person or group committing the crime "shall be punished, whether they are constitutionally responsible rulers, public officials or private individuals."

But the treaty does not dictate the outcome of a genocide conviction. Past sentences have ranged from 10 months to life in prison, depending on the person's role in the crime.

If national courts in countries that have signed the treaty fail to prosecute individuals, the International Criminal Court in The Hague is supposed to step in.

But the International Criminal Court has no authority to arrest on its own and must rely on the cooperation of individual nations to enforce punishment.

Using the term genocide also has political implications. On April 28, 1994, a reporter asked U.S. State Department spokeswoman Christine Shelley whether the events in Rwanda could be considered a genocide.

Earlier that month, the Rwandan Armed Forces and Hutu militia had begun a violent and deliberate campaign to kill Tutsi and moderate Hutu politicians. Thousands of people were killed on the first day.

But Shelley stopped short of calling the situation in Rwanda a genocide. She responded by saying the United States needed more evidence to determine whether the situation met the U.N. definition.

At the time, Molly Williamson, the deputy assistant secretary of defense for Middle East/Africa, also warned against using the term genocide to describe the events in Rwanda, because, according to a Defense Department discussion paper, a "genocide finding could commit [the U.S.] to actually 'do something.'"

What About Myanmar?

When it comes to Myanmar, many of the same concerns apply.

In October 2016, former President Barack Obama issued an executive order to lift economic sanctions on Myanmar after what his administration said were positive steps in addressing human rights abuses in the country following the election of activist and Nobel Prize winner Aung San Suu Kyi's party.

"I have determined that the situation that gave rise to the national emergency with respect to Burma has been significantly altered by Burma's substantial advances to promote democracy, including historic elections in November 2015," Obama wrote in an October 2016 letter to Congress.

Silk said the Obama administration avoided using the word genocide in part because that would undermine a "hopeful democracy and its leader, and there is general hesitation on the part of powerful states to use the word genocide and trigger legal and moral obligations."

Joshua Kurlantzick, a senior fellow for Southeast Asia at the Council on Foreign Relations, said the United States is unlikely to call the situation in Myanmar a genocide before other experts or the U.N. says it first.

Senior U.N. officials appear to be hesitant to criticize Suu Kyi, fearing that it would risk efforts to guide the country through a political transition from military rule to democracy and destabilize the U.N.'s relief efforts in the country.

And the U.N. cannot determine genocidal intent without an independent commission of inquiry or fact-finding procedure. A commission of inquiry cannot begin investigating without U.N. Security Council approval. But without cooperation from the Myanmar government, investigators would not be allowed into the country.

In the case of the Rwandan genocide, more than 20 years later, many of the perpetrators have been brought to justice in Rwandan courts or domestic courts in Europe and North America. But this is the result of an intentional effort by the Rwandan government.

Unilaterally, Kurlantzick said there is limited opportunity for the United States to change the situation in Myanmar.

"They could push for more aid or for the United Nations to have access to the Rakhine state, but they can't impose U.N. Security Council sanctions because there are countries within the council that don't support that," he said.

Declaring the violence a genocide would force the international community's hand, Silk said. Once a genocide is declared, he added, doing nothing is no longer an option.

The international community's responsibility under international law does not change based on whether a situation is determined a crime against humanity or a genocide, said Tasnim Motala, a lawyer and co-author of a paper by the Lowenstein International Human Rights Clinic at Yale Law School, which found a "strong foundation from which to infer genocidal intent by security forces, government officials, local Rakhine, and others."

The Responsibility to Protect doctrine says that if a state is unable to protect its own populations from "genocide, war crimes, ethnic cleansing and crimes against humanity" then the international community must do something.

But again, international law cannot be enforced without support from both individual states and the international community, Motala said. "International law lacks enforcement mechanisms, it demands buy in from an international community. Clearly it hasn't been effective," she said.

Viewpoint 2

> *"The Convention on the Prevention and Punishment of the Crime of Genocide (Genocide Convention) is an instrument of international law that codified for the first time the crime of genocide."*

What Is the Genocide Convention of 1948?

Climate Change Trust

In the following viewpoint, the Climate Change Trust examines and defines the Genocide Convention of 1948. The Climate Change Trust outlines the Genocide Convention and explains how the crime of genocide is defined and how it is punished. It also considers how climate and climate change factor into genocide by looking at man-made famine and the deaths and displacement of people due to extreme weather events caused by climate change. The Climate Change Trust is a not-for-profit, nonpolitical organization that exists to offer help and assistance to anyone searching for technological solutions or policy revision related to the issue of climate change.

As you read, consider the following questions:

1. According to the viewpoint, when did the UN General Assembly first recognize genocide as an international crime?

2. When does genocide take place, as reported by the author?
3. As of 2019, had all countries signed on to the Genocide Convention, based on the information in this viewpoint?

The Genocide Convention was conceived largely in response to World War II, which saw atrocities such as the Holocaust that lacked an adequate description or legal definition. Polish-Jewish lawyer Raphael Lemkin, who had coined the term genocide in 1944 to describe Nazi policies in occupied Europe, campaigned for its recognition as a crime under international law. This culminated in 1946 in a landmark resolution by the General Assembly that recognized genocide as an international crime and called for the creation of a binding treaty to prevent and punish its perpetration. Subsequent discussions and negotiations among UN member states resulted in the CPPCG.

The CPPCG has influenced law at both the national and international level. Its definition of genocide has been adopted by international and hybrid tribunals, such as the International Criminal Court, and incorporated into the domestic law of several countries. Its provisions are widely considered to be reflective of customary law and therefore binding on all nations whether or not they are parties. The International Court of Justice has likewise ruled that the principles underlying the Convention represent a peremptory norm against genocide that no government can derogate.

The Convention on the Prevention and Punishment of the Crime of Genocide (Genocide Convention) is an instrument of international law that codified for the first time the crime of genocide. The Genocide Convention was the first human rights treaty adopted by the General Assembly of the United Nations on 9 December 1948 and signified the international community's commitment to 'never again' after the atrocities committed during the Second World War. Its adoption marked a crucial step towards the development of international human rights and international criminal law as we know it today.

According to the Genocide Convention, genocide is a crime that can take place both in time of war as well as in time of peace. The definition of the crime of genocide, as set out in the Convention, has been widely adopted at both national and international levels, including in the 1998 Rome Statute of the International Criminal Court (ICC). Learn more about the definition of the crime of genocide.

Importantly, the Convention establishes on State Parties the obligation to take measures to prevent and to punish the crime of genocide, including by enacting relevant legislation and punishing perpetrators, "whether they are constitutionally responsible rulers, public officials or private individuals" (Article IV). That obligation, in addition to the prohibition not to commit genocide, have been considered as norms of international customary law and therefore, binding on all States, whether or not they have ratified the Genocide Convention.

Status of Membership

The Genocide Convention has been ratified or acceded to by 152 States (as of July 2019). Other 42 United Nations Member States have yet to do so. From those, 19 are from Africa, 17 from Asia and 6 from America.

The Special Advisor on the Prevention of Genocide calls upon all United Nations Member States that are not yet party to the Genocide Convention, to ratify or accede to it as a matter of priority, so that the Genocide Convention becomes an instrument of universal membership.

International Day

Every year on 9 December, the United Nations marks the adoption of the Genocide Convention, which is also the International Day of Commemoration and Dignity of the Victims of the Crime of Genocide and of the Prevention of this Crime. Watch the latest event marking the 70th anniversary of the Convention.

Convention on the Prevention and Punishment of the Crime of Genocide

Approved and proposed for signature and ratification or accession by General Assembly resolution 260 A (III) of 9 December 1948

Entry into force: 12 January 1951, in accordance with article XIII

The Contracting Parties,

Having considered the declaration made by the General Assembly of the United Nations in its resolution 96 (I) dated 11 December 1946 that genocide is a crime under international law, contrary to the spirit and aims of the United Nations and condemned by the civilized world,

Recognizing that at all periods of history genocide has inflicted great losses on humanity, and

Being convinced that, in order to liberate mankind from such an odious scourge, international co-operation is required,

Hereby agree as hereinafter provided:

Article I

The Contracting Parties confirm that genocide, whether committed in time of peace or in time of war, is a crime under international law which they undertake to prevent and to punish.

Article II

In the present Convention, genocide means any of the following acts committed with intent to destroy, in whole or in part, a national, ethnical, racial or religious group, as such:

(a) Killing members of the group;

(b) Causing serious bodily or mental harm to members of the group;

(c) Deliberately inflicting on the group conditions of life calculated to bring about its physical destruction in whole or in part;

(d) Imposing measures intended to prevent births within the group;

(e) Forcibly transferring children of the group to another group.

Article III
The following acts shall be punishable:

(a) Genocide;
(b) Conspiracy to commit genocide;
(c) Direct and public incitement to commit genocide;
(d) Attempt to commit genocide;
(e) Complicity in genocide.

Article IV
Persons committing genocide or any of the other acts enumerated in article III shall be punished, whether they are constitutionally responsible rulers, public officials or private individuals.

Article V
The Contracting Parties undertake to enact, in accordance with their respective Constitutions, the necessary legislation to give effect to the provisions of the present Convention, and, in particular, to provide effective penalties for persons guilty of genocide or any of the other acts enumerated in article III.

Article VI
Persons charged with genocide or any of the other acts enumerated in article III shall be tried by a competent tribunal of the State in the territory of which the act was committed, or by such international penal tribunal as may have jurisdiction with respect to those Contracting Parties which shall have accepted its jurisdiction.

Article VII
Genocide and the other acts enumerated in article III shall not be considered as political crimes for the purpose of extradition.

The Contracting Parties pledge themselves in such cases to grant extradition in accordance with their laws and treaties in force.

Article VIII

Any Contracting Party may call upon the competent organs of the United Nations to take such action under the Charter of the United Nations as they consider appropriate for the prevention and suppression of acts of genocide or any of the other acts enumerated in article III.

Article IX

Disputes between the Contracting Parties relating to the interpretation, application or fulfilment of the present Convention, including those relating to the responsibility of a State for genocide or for any of the other acts enumerated in article III, shall be submitted to the International Court of Justice at the request of any of the parties to the dispute.

Article X

The present Convention, of which the Chinese, English, French, Russian and Spanish texts are equally authentic, shall bear the date of 9 December 1948.

Article XI

The present Convention shall be open until 31 December 1949 for signature on behalf of any Member of the United Nations and of any non-member State to which an invitation to sign has been addressed by the General Assembly.

The present Convention shall be ratified, and the instruments of ratification shall be deposited with the Secretary-General of the United Nations.

After 1 January 1950, the present Convention may be acceded to on behalf of any Member of the United Nations and of any non-member State which has received an invitation as aforesaid.

Instruments of accession shall be deposited with the Secretary-General of the United Nations.

Article XII

Any Contracting Party may at any time, by notification addressed to the Secretary-General of the United Nations, extend the application of the present Convention to all or any of the territories for the conduct of whose foreign relations that Contracting Party is responsible.

Article XIII

On the day when the first twenty instruments of ratification or accession have been deposited, the Secretary-General shall draw up a procès-verbal and transmit a copy thereof to each Member of the United Nations and to each of the non-member States contemplated in article XI.

The present Convention shall come into force on the ninetieth day following the date of deposit of the twentieth instrument of ratification or accession.

Any ratification or accession effected subsequent to the latter date shall become effective on the ninetieth day following the deposit of the instrument of ratification or accession.

Article XIV

The present Convention shall remain in effect for a period of ten years as from the date of its coming into force.

It shall thereafter remain in force for successive periods of five years for such Contracting Parties as have not denounced it at least six months before the expiration of the current period.

Denunciation shall be effected by a written notification addressed to the Secretary-General of the United Nations.

Article XV

If, as a result of denunciations, the number of Parties to the present Convention should become less than sixteen, the Convention shall cease to be in force as from the date on which the last of these denunciations shall become effective.

Article XVI

A request for the revision of the present Convention may be made at any time by any Contracting Party by means of a notification in writing addressed to the Secretary-General.

The General Assembly shall decide upon the steps, if any, to be taken in respect of such request.

Article XVII

The Secretary-General of the United Nations shall notify all Members of the United Nations and the non-member States contemplated in article XI of the following:

(a) Signatures, ratifications and accessions received in accordance with article XI;

(b) Notifications received in accordance with article XII;

(c) The date upon which the present Convention comes into force in accordance with article XIII;

(d) Denunciations received in accordance with article XIV;

(e) The abrogation of the Convention in accordance with article XV;

(f) Notifications received in accordance with article XVI.

Article XVIII

The original of the present Convention shall be deposited in the archives of the United Nations.

A certified copy of the Convention shall be transmitted to each Member of the United Nations and to each of the non-member States contemplated in article XI.

Article XIX

The present Convention shall be registered by the Secretary-General of the United Nations on the date of its coming into force.

Man Made Famine

There is little difference between Man Made Famine, once the cause of the starvation and deaths is known, than other forms of genocide. Those responsible are held to be Climate Nazis by many, and may one day be accountable for such crimes in the International Criminal Court.

Man Made Famine is a form of geographical genocide. You don't have to line people up and shoot them, gas, or otherwise take their lives to commit the crime of this form of genocide. You simply have to carry on, business as usual, in the knowledge that failing to take action to curb global warming, is killing people in another land.

Famine that is caused by the industrialization and acceleration of growth of economies in unsustainable fashion, is nothing less than the premeditated murder of those less fortunate peoples in climate vulnerable locations on planet earth, who are unable to defend themselves.

Global Warming

The cause of much famine is man-made. As our climate warms, the artic ice melts causing ocean levels to rise and agricultural land to become deserts. The most influential world leaders, of the G7 and G20 are fully aware of the consequences of failing to act in sufficient time to prevent Geographical Genocide. According to the 1948 Convention, Genocide is a crime. Any person or state advocating policies that do not seek to reduce climate warming, are therefore criminals. The excuse that their economy might suffer, is no excuse when it comes to (in effect) murdering another human being. It is the insatiable lust for economic growth that has caused the deaths of millions of displaced persons and those who died of lung cancer.

VIEWPOINT 3

> *"On 24 March 2017, the UN Human Rights Council agreed to form an independent fact-finding mission on Myanmar."*

How Genocide Was Investigated in Myanmar

Roland Hughes

In the following viewpoint, Roland Hughes presents evidence of a genocide in Myanmar. Step by step, Hughes outlines and reports on the investigation leading up to this decision. He presents statistics and reasons why the investigating committee firmly decided that this was a case of genocide. Finally, he explains how the law applies to this situation and the next steps involved in holding those responsible accountable. Roland Hughes is a weekend editor for Apple and formerly was an assistant editor for BBC News, which broadcasts news and current affairs in the United Kingdom and around the world.

As you read, consider the following questions:

1. According to Hughes, which group of people were targeted for genocide in Myanmar?
2. What evidence is there that genocide occurred in Myanmar, according to Hughes?

"Myanmar Rohingya: How a 'genocide' was investigated," by Roland Hughes, BBC, September 3, 2018. Reprinted by permission.

3. Who was condemned in the investigation, and who should face prosecution, according to the viewpoint?

Indiscriminate killing; villages burned to the ground; children assaulted; women gang-raped - these are the findings of United Nations investigators who allege that "the gravest crimes under international law" were committed in Myanmar last August.

Such was their severity, the report said, the army must be investigated for genocide against the Rohingya Muslims in the western Rakhine state.

The investigators' conclusions came despite them not being granted access to Myanmar by the government there, which has since rejected the report.

This is how the investigators came to their conclusions.

The Build-Up

On 24 March 2017, the UN Human Rights Council agreed to form an independent fact-finding mission on Myanmar to look into "alleged recent human rights violations by military and security forces."

Five months after the mission was formed, Myanmar's army launched a major assault on Rakhine state, following deadly attacks by Rohingya militants on police posts.

The military's campaign became the main focus of the investigation, which also looked into rights abuses in Kachin and Shan states.

The mission wrote to Myanmar's government three times asking for access to the country. It received no response.

The Interviews

"The first rule was 'do no harm,'" says Christopher Sidoti, one of the three people who headed the investigation.

"Those people we spoke to had been heavily traumatised, and if our staff considered that an interview would be re-traumatising, it wouldn't have been conducted.

"No evidence is so important that it warrants re-traumatising someone who has gone through all these experiences.

At least 725,000 people have fled Rakhine state over the past 12 months, many to neighbouring Bangladesh. As a result, despite not getting access to Myanmar, investigators were able to gather a vast amount of testimony from people who had experienced violence at first-hand before fleeing.

They spoke to 875 people in Bangladesh, Malaysia, Thailand, Indonesia and the UK, and made a decision early on that the most valuable testimony would come from people who had not shared their stories before.

"We didn't want to interview people who had been interviewed by other organisations," Mr Sidoti, an Australian human rights law expert, says. "We didn't want a situation where people's evidence could have been tainted.

"We tried to get people from a wide variety of areas and when we became more and more focused later on, we would deliberately, through a community network, seek out others from that area to get a better picture of what went on."

The Evidence

"We would never use just one account as proof," Mr Sidoti says. "We always sought corroboration from primary and secondary sources."

Those sources included videos, photographs, documents and satellite images, which showed the destruction of Rohingya villages over several months in 2017.

In one case, investigators had received several reports from refugees in Cox's Bazar, Bangladesh, that a village had been destroyed in particular circumstances at a particular time.

Investigators were then able to source satellite images that corroborated what witnesses had said.

Satellites images showed that:

- About 392 villages were partially or totally destroyed in northern Rakhine state

- Close to 40% of all homes in the area—37,700 buildings—were affected
- About 80% were burned in the first three weeks of the military campaign

Getting hold of photographic evidence from the ground proved to be more of a challenge.

"When people were leaving Rakhine state, they were being stopped, searched and deprived of their money, gold and mobile phones," Mr Sidoti says. "It seemed pretty clear this was an attempt to get video or photographic evidence they had recorded.

"There wasn't much left but we made use of it."

The Accused

The report names six senior military figures it believes should go on trial, including Commander-in-Chief Min Aung Hlaing and his deputy.

How were investigators able to point the finger directly at these men?

The case here is not based on a paper trail, or a recording, but instead on research.

Investigators relied heavily on others' detailed understanding of how Myanmar's government works. Among them was a military adviser who had co-operated with war crimes tribunals in the past.

"We have been able to access extraordinary international advice on various aspects of Myanmar's military," Mr Sidoti says. "The conclusion we have come up with is that the army is so tightly controlled that nothing happens involving the army in Myanmar without the commander-in-chief and his deputies knowing."

While the people believed to have given the orders have been named, work is ongoing to identify the members of the military who may have committed atrocities.

"We do have a list of alleged perpetrators on the ground and they will remain confidential for now," Mr Sidoti says. "Their names have come up frequently enough for them to be put on lists to face more investigation."

The Law

Identifying what appears to be genocide and proving that what happened fits the legal definition of genocide are two different things.

"Evidence of crimes against humanity was very quickly obtained and was quite overwhelming," Mr Sidoti says. "Genocide is a much more legally complex issue."

As the report states, genocide is when "a person commits a prohibited act with the intent to destroy, in whole or in part, a national, ethnical, racial or religious group."

The key word is "intent." Investigators believe the evidence of that intent by the Myanmar army is clear.

They cite statements by commanders and suspected perpetrators, and the degree of planning required to carry out such an operation. But still, identifying a genocide from a legal perspective took a significant amount of legal work.

"We arrived at a position we had not expected to be in when we were beginning," Mr Sidoti says. "None of the three of us thought the evidence for genocide would be as strong as it was. That came as a surprise."

The Next Step

The report says that the six military officials should face trial. It also condemns Myanmar's de facto leader, Nobel Peace Prize laureate Aung San Suu Kyi, for failing to intervene to stop attacks, and the UN's outgoing rights chief this week said she should have resigned as a result.

The report also makes a series of recommendations, including the referral of the investigation to the International Criminal Court or to a new tribunal, and the imposition of an arms embargo.

However, China has so far resisted strong action against its neighbour and ally Myanmar on the UN Security Council, where it holds a veto.

Mr Sidoti acknowledges that officials in Myanmar are unlikely to investigate the allegations themselves. Last year, an internal investigation by the army exonerated itself of blame in the Rohingya crisis, and Myanmar's Permanent Representative to the UN last week told BBC Burmese the report was full of "one-sided accusations against us."

"We have made recommendations and it is up to others to act on them," Mr Sidoti says. "I have a high expectation that the Security Council will act on its responsibilities. But I'm not naive."

Viewpoint 4

> *"War crimes also often take place in tandem with other atrocity crimes – a legal term that also encompasses ethnic cleansing, crimes against humanity and genocide."*

Ukrainians Suffer at the Hands of Russia

Alexander Hinton

In the following viewpoint, Alexander Hinton contends that, at the time this viewpoint was published in April 2022, it seemed very likely that Russia would commit genocide in Ukraine. Hinton analyzes the situation in Ukraine, comparing what happened there to other instances of countries that have suffered from genocide in the past. Hinton provides multiple examples comparing Russia's tactics in Ukraine to other instances of genocide, drawing a strong connection between them and the situation in Ukraine. Alexander Hinton is a distinguished professor and director of the Center for the Study of Genocide and Human Rights at Rutgers University in Newark, New Jersey.

As you read, consider the following questions:

1. Has Russia committed war crimes in Ukraine, as reported in the viewpoint?

"Is Russia committing genocide in Ukraine? A human rights expert looks at the warning signs," by Alexander Hinton, The Conversation, April 1, 2022. https://theconversation.com/is-russia-committing-genocide-in-ukraine-a-human-rights-expert-looks-at-the-warning-signs-180017.

2. As stated in the viewpoint, do experts agree on whether Ukraine is under a genocidal attack by the Russians?
3. What are two pieces of evidence that indicate that genocide is occurring in Ukraine, according to the author?

There's a real threat that Russia will commit genocide in Ukraine. As evidence of war crimes emerges, there is reason to believe it may already be taking place.

"Russia's forces have committed war crimes in Ukraine," U.S. Secretary of State Antony Blinken said in a statement on March 23, 2022. Blinken cited as evidence for his allegation Russia's destruction of "apartment buildings, schools, hospitals, critical infrastructure" and a maternity hospital in the besieged city of Mariupol that was marked with the Russian word for children.

Russia has killed at least 1,189 civilians and wounded 1,901 additional Ukrainians since it began its attack on Ukraine in February 2022, according to the United Nations. This actual death toll is likely much higher.

Such attacks on civilians during conflict are considered war crimes under international law.

But war crimes also often take place in tandem with other atrocity crimes—a legal term that also encompasses ethnic cleansing, crimes against humanity and genocide.

And indeed, there is evidence Russia has also committed crimes against humanity, or widespread attacks against Ukraine's civilian population. Such attacks include killings, enforced disappearances, rape and torture.

These also include the mass deportations of Ukrainians into Russia that the Kremlin is reportedly carrying out in eastern Ukraine.

Some observers warn that this violence has the potential to become genocidal, particularly given Russian propaganda and physical destruction of Mariupol and other cities.

Ukrainian officials claim genocide has already begun. "The aerial bombing of a children's hospital," President Volodymyr Zelenskyy said on March 9, 2022, "is the ultimate evidence that genocide of Ukrainians is happening."

Other experts disagree, sometimes arguing that the Russian violence doesn't meet the legal requirements of genocide.

Given the scale of Russian violence in Ukraine, however, genocide warnings need to be taken seriously.

The field of genocide studies, in which I have long worked, has developed frameworks for assessing the threat of genocide in such volatile situations. These tools, including one used by the U.N., indicate Ukraine is indeed at considerable risk for genocide.

Historical Precedent

Genocide refers to "acts committed with intent to destroy, in whole or in part, a national, ethnical, racial or religious group."

These acts involve not just killing people, but seeking to destroy the target group by causing "serious bodily or mental harm," creating harsh "conditions of life," preventing births and "forcibly transferring" children to another group.

One predictor for genocide is a history of mass human rights violations and atrocity crimes, including genocide.

Russia has a long history of mass violence against Ukrainians and other groups.

Perhaps most infamously, the Soviet Union enacted land policies that prompted a food shortage and a famine, killing millions of Ukrainians from 1932 to 1933. This is known as the Holodomor, a Ukrainian word meaning "death by hunger."

Other Soviet atrocities include forced deportation of national and ethnic groups and massive political purges.

After the Soviet Union collapsed in 1991, Russia committed mass violence against civilians in Chechnya, Georgia and Syria. It bombarded and obliterated cities like Grozny in 1995 and Aleppo in 2016.

Political Upheaval

Genocide and atrocity crimes are also strongly correlated with political upheaval, especially war. Such upheaval destabilizes a society and makes it less secure—especially for vulnerable groups of people who may be blamed for the political or economic instability.

Genocide has taken place during global conflicts, as illustrated by the Armenian genocide during World War I, and the Holocaust during World War II.

And then there are genocides associated with colonial conquest and invasion, like the destruction of Indigenous peoples in North America.

Such countries as China and Cambodia have also undertaken social engineering projects resulting in genocide.

Russia has experienced a number of political upheavals, including a current economic crisis. Russia's invasion of Ukraine is the sort of armed conflict often associated with atrocity crimes.

Ideology and Demonization

Genocide is justified by propaganda and language that devalues and demonizes target populations. Historical examples abound, ranging from European colonial caricatures of Indigenous "brutes" and "savages" to Nazi representations of Jews as rats.

Russia is using this type of demonizing language to justify its invasion of Ukraine. First, Russia depicts its violence as necessary to "denazify" Ukraine. President Vladimir Putin, for example, has referred to the Ukrainian leadership as a far-right "gang of drug addicts and neo-Nazis."

And second, Putin has suggested that Ukrainian identity is not real and that, historically, "Russians and Ukrainians are one people—one nation, in fact."

Proving genocidal intent is difficult, especially in a court of law. This is evident in current debates—including an ongoing court case at the International Court of Justice—about whether Myanmar committed genocide against the Rohingya people, a Muslim minority group.

But it can be inferred by patterns of violence consistent with the legal definition of genocide.

Has Russia Carried Out Genocidal Acts?

Russia has targeted and killed civilians and reportedly forcibly deported hundreds of thousands of Ukrainians, including children, to Russia. It has bombed a maternity hospital.

Russia has also created “harsh conditions of life” in parts of Ukraine. It has destroyed electrical and water supplies, deprived Ukrainians of food and humanitarian aid and displaced more than 10 million people within and outside of Ukraine.

Russia seeks to seize and Russify Donbas and other parts of eastern Ukraine, where, if Putin is taken at his word, an “imaginary” Ukrainian identity will be erased.

There is a significant risk that Russia will commit genocide in Ukraine. It is possible that a genocide has already begun.

Viewpoint 5

> *"While recognizing the horror of the atrocities being carried out by Russia in Ukraine, U.S. national security adviser Jake Sullivan said Monday that he had not seen evidence they had risen to the level of genocide."*

The U.S. Is Careful to Distinguish War Crimes from Genocide in Russia's Invasion of Ukraine

Haley Ott

As this viewpoint by Haley Ott explains, in April 2022 the U.S. formally accused Russia of committing war crimes in its invasion of Ukraine. This viewpoint considers what war crimes are, pointing out that deliberate attacks on civilians or indiscriminate attacks that end up killing many civilians are considered war crimes. However, the challenge in investigating war crimes is connecting the actions of troops with military and political leadership to prove that these attacks are being ordered by leaders. Ott also explains that whether the invasion of Ukraine should be considered genocide is a point of contention in the international community. Haley Ott is a multimedia journalist for CBS News.

As you read, consider the following questions:

"What are war crimes, is Russia committing them in Ukraine, and could Putin be prosecuted?" by Haley Ott, CBS News, April 5, 2022. Reprinted by permission.

1. Where are violations of the legal standards for warfare prosecuted?
2. Can national governments investigate war crimes, according to this viewpoint?
3. According to this viewpoint, did it seem likely that Putin would be tried for war crimes at the time of publication?

As horrific scenes were revealed in the wake of Russian troops pulling out of the town of Bucha in Ukraine, President Joe Biden on Monday accused Russian President Vladimir Putin of war crimes.

"He is a war criminal," Mr. Biden said. "I think it is a war crime. . . . He should be held accountable."

The United States had already formally accused Russian forces of committing war crimes in Ukraine, and a number of national and international organizations have opened investigations, collecting evidence to build cases. But could Putin himself ever face a war crimes trial?

What Are War Crimes?

There are a number of international treaties—the Geneva Convention and the Geneva Protocol being two of the most important—that establish international legal standards for warfare. Any violation of those standards is a war crime that can be prosecuted at the International Criminal Court (ICC) in the Hague, and can result in imprisonment for perpetrators.

National governments, unilaterally or in partnerships, can also conduct their own war crimes investigations and prosecutions based on their own laws or the principle of universal jurisdiction, which determines some war crimes to be so extraordinary that they shock the conscience of humanity as a whole and therefore can be prosecuted anywhere.

Deliberate attacks against civilians are war crimes, as are "methods of war that are inherently indiscriminate and that simply can't make the distinction between the civilian population and armed forces," Jim Goldston, executive director of the Open Society Foundations' Justice Initiative, told CBS News.

Goldston said there were many indications that Russia was committing war crimes in Ukraine.

"There is an enormous effort now underway … to kind of hoover up all this information and organize it, that looks at where military forces are located, what are the targets, what are the structures being targeted, and gathering that together with testimonies that are being reported of people who are being victimized in these areas," he said.

All of the information being gathered could be used as evidence in possible war crimes trials at the ICC or in separate tribunals.

"One of the challenges in these kinds of investigations, though, will be to demonstrate the linkage between what is happening on the ground and those who have military or political responsibility for ordering these attacks," Goldston said.

Is Russia Committing Genocide in Ukraine?

Ukraine's president Volodymyr Zelenskyy has called Russia's actions in Ukraine "genocide," appealing to nations around the world for help.

"The aerial bombing of a children's hospital is the ultimate evidence that genocide of Ukrainians is happening," Zelenskyy said on March 9.

But while recognizing the horror of the atrocities being carried out by Russia in Ukraine, U.S. national security adviser Jake Sullivan said Monday that he had not seen evidence they had risen to the level of genocide.

Under international law, genocide is defined as "acts committed with intent to destroy, in whole or in part, a national, ethnical, racial or religious group." This can involve killing or causing serious bodily harm to members of the group, deliberately inflicting conditions of life designed to destroy the group, forcibly removing children from the group and transferring them to others, or imposing measures intended to prevent births in the group.

Whether Russia's actions in Ukraine amount to genocide is still being debated by experts, Professor Alex Hinton, director of the Center for the Study of Genocide and Human Rights at Rutgers University, wrote in *The Conversation*. Russia has targeted and killed civilians and created "harsh conditions of life" in many parts of Ukraine, including the besieged city of Mariupol, where civilians without food or water continue to be denied access to lifesaving aid shipments. It has also reportedly forcibly transported hundreds of Ukrainians, including children, to Russia. In public rhetoric, it has undermined and denied the very existence of Ukrainian identity and outlined a goal eradicating it in some areas.

"There is a significant risk that Russia will commit genocide in Ukraine," Hinton wrote. "It is possible that a genocide has already begun."

Could Putin Be Tried for War Crimes?

"Traditionally in the international criminal tribunals, it has been very difficult to take [war crimes and crimes against humanity] all the way up to the top," Philippe Sands, a law professor and Director of the Center on International Courts and Tribunals at University College London told CBS News' partner network, BBC News.

Sands is among a number academics and former world leaders calling for the establishment of a special international tribunal modeled on the Nuremberg Trials, which were held for Nazi leaders after World War II, to hold Russia's leaders to account for the crime of "aggression" in Ukraine.

"A crime of aggression is waging an illegal war," Sands said. "It's part of international law, it's part of the law of Ukraine, and it's pretty clearly established in the present case, because there's no justification."

In the case of Russia's invasion of Ukraine—barring an extremely unlikely referral from the United Nations Security Council, where Russia holds veto power—the ICC does not have jurisdiction over the crime of aggression, so a separate tribunal would be necessary for any indictment. But because it is the act of waging an illegal war, it could be easier to attribute it to Putin himself.

"The crime of aggression is virtually, by definition, a leadership crime," Goldston said. "Only leaders have the power to actually invade another state, or a small circle of folks around them who have the political authority to actually make that happen."

If such a case did get off the ground, it's still unclear whether Putin himself could be successfully prosecuted, or what an indictment might mean for him.

"What happens if there were a tribunal that were to indict him? It would face challenges. One, of head of state immunity. The law on the immunity of someone who's head of state is debated, certainly, depending on the jurisdiction that is bringing the charges. And then, just the physical question of how you would get custody over somebody like that is huge," Goldston said.

"But there are damaging effects of indictment, short of custody," Goldston added. Pointing to the indictments of the former political and military leaders of the Bosnian Serbs, he said: "The indictments themselves, the public nature of the charges, I think it's fair to say, acted to stigmatize them, to isolate them politically, to make it untenable for them to participate in political negotiations and diplomatic negotiations. So indictments alone can have an effect, even short of arrest."

Periodical and Internet Sources Bibliography

The following articles have been selected to supplement the diverse views presented in this chapter.

Katrin Bennhold, "80 Years Ago the Nazis Planned the 'Final Solution.' It took 90 Minutes," *New York Times*, January 20, 2022. https://www.nytimes.com/2022/01/20/world/europe/lake-wannsee-conference-final-solution-holocaust.html.

Rehman Chishti, "Now is the Time to Recognize the Genocide in Burma," Atlantic Council, September 17, 2021. https://www.atlanticcouncil.org/blogs/new-atlanticist/now-is-the-time-to-recognize-the-genocide-in-burma/.

Nell Clark, "An Expert Says It May Be Hard, But Not Impossible, To Prove Genocide in Ukraine," NPR, April 12, 2022. https://www.npr.org/2022/04/12/1092317791/ukraine-russia-ethnic-cleansing.

Robert Coalson, "What's the Difference Between Crimes Against Humanity and Genocide?" the *Atlantic*, March 19, 2013. https://www.theatlantic.com/international/archive/2013/03/whats-the-difference-between-crimes-against-humanity-and-genocide/274167/.

Gregory G. Dimijian, "Warfare, Genocide, and Ethnic Conflict: A Darwinian Approach," NIH, July 23, 2010. https://www.ncbi.nlm.nih.gov/pmc/articles/PMC2900985/.

Jaakko Heiskanen, "In the Shadow of Genocide: Ethnocide, Ethnic Cleansing, and International Order," *Global Studies Quarterly*, October 1, 2021. https://academic.oup.com/isagsq/article/1/4/ksab030/6380106.

Sahar Khan, "Ethnic Cleansing vs. Genocide: The Politics Behind Labeling the Rohingya Crisis," Cato Institute, November 29, 2017. https://www.cato.org/blog/ethnic-cleansing-vs-genocide-politics-behind-labeling-rohingya-crisis.

Pia Krishnankutty, "Pogrom, Genocide & Ethnic Cleansing: What These Mean and How They Differ From Each Other," ThePrint, February 28, 2020. https://theprint.in/theprint-essential/pogrom-genocide-ethnic-cleansing-what-these-mean-and-how-they-differ-from-each-other/372680/.

Ashish Kumar Sen, "Is Russia Committing Genocide in Ukraine?" United States Institute of Peace, September 21, 2022. https://www.usip.org/publications/2022/09/russia-committing-genocide-ukraine.

Caysi Simpson, "The Difference Between Ethnic Cleansing and Genocide," the Borgen Project, February 13, 2018. https://borgenproject.org/difference-ethnic-cleansing-and-genocide/.

OPPOSING VIEWPOINTS® SERIES

Chapter 2

How Does Racism Relate to Acts of Mass Brutality?

Chapter Preface

According to the United States Holocaust Memorial Museum, there are a number of large-scale crimes that are committed against populations of people. These include genocide, mass killing, ethnic cleansing, war crimes, and crimes against humanity. Studies of past violence against groups of people have shown that there are certain risk factors or warning signs that may precede these acts of violence. But are the causes of mass brutality always the same?

Think about what might happen if governmental leaders would learn from the examples of mass violence throughout history. Could modern-day brutality be prevented? It's most likely safe to say that ordinary citizens caught up in this violence would like leaders to avoid large scale crimes, which makes understanding the risk factors for mass violence and detecting patterns in these atrocities particularly important. One of the key factors in acts of brutality against another group of people is the concept of "othering," or treating a group of people as fundamentally different and separate from yourself and people like you. This is also a key variable in racism, so it comes as no surprise that the two are often related.

The viewpoints in this chapter explore different instances, both historical and recent, of mass brutality caused by racism and analyze its causes. They will expand their knowledge about the effects of racism against Black Americans and Indigenous Americans and how this has led to mass brutality. They will learn about and understand the Tulsa race massacre (1921), in which Black residents of the Greenwood District of Tulsa, Oklahoma, were subjected to racial violence at the hands of mobs. They will also gain an understanding of the Indian Removal Act, which was signed into law by then-President Andrew Jackson in 1830 and forced Native Americans living in U.S. territories to move west of the Mississippi River in what would become known as the Trail of Tears. In recent years, these acts have come to be considered instances of ethnic cleansing, and some historians have even regarded the forced removal of Native Americans and the enslavement of Black Americans as instances of genocide.

Not surprisingly, the cause of racism and mass brutality is a complex issue. The authors in this chapter debate and inform readers about this important topic.

Viewpoint 1

> *"The hatred of the physicality, cultures and identities of 'othered' groups is a global phenomenon."*

Violence and Racism Are Related, and One Affects the Other

Sarah Malotane Henkeman

In the following viewpoint, Sarah Malotane Henkeman explains the concept of the intertwined relationship between racism and violence. Henkeman maintains that racism is systemic, and its effects persist over generations. In racism there is a sense of "othering" one group and dehumanizing people in this group. It causes the sense of one group's superiority and the other's inferiority to be internalized, which enables racism to be resilient and cause intergenerational harm. Sarah Malotane Henkeman is a senior staff associate in the law faculty at the University of Cape Town in South Africa and is a researcher of social justice.

As you read, consider the following questions:

1. According to Henkeman, how did Black Lives Matter get started?
2. What is symbolic violence, as explained by the author?
3. What are the multiple and simultaneous effects of racism, as stated in the viewpoint?

Racism is a form of both visible and invisible violence. Veteran peace researcher Johan Galtung has shown that violence is cultural, structural and direct. This triad was adapted in South Africa as interlinked symbolic, structural, psychological and physical violence against "otherness."

This conceptual framework can be applied to direct and indirect experiences of racism, as well as to other forms of violence. The most recent manifestation of these has been the outcry over black hair. Some referred to it as a hair war. It revealed a cumulative visceral, tacit and explicit knowledge of racism as violence.

The hatred of the physicality, cultures and identities of "othered" groups is a global phenomenon. America's Black Lives Matter movement arose out of the deaths of black people because blackness has effectively been criminalised. The "animalisation" of blackness has its roots in slavery.

States do not record the structural violence of racism as part of crime statistics. But this invisible violence has driven some people to self-harm. It has masked forms of suicide. It shortens lives and kills babies.

Internalised white superiority and internalised black inferiority remain resilient in South Africa. This is despite resistance to racism over centuries. It begs the question: after 22 years of democracy, what have most of colonialism and apartheid's beneficiaries done to understand these evils? What have they done to delink from them, and to dismantle racism?

A "Post-Conflict" Society

The end of apartheid in 1994 only interrupted racism at a political level. It did not automatically turn South Africa into the "post-conflict society" many claim it is.

In this sense, feminist writers Pumla Gqola and Pumla Gobodo-Madikizela help us to think differently about violence.

They look beyond visible manifestations of violence in their analyses of physical violence (rape, bodily harm and murder). They show violence also to be symbolic (othering), structural (patriarchy, economic inequality) and psychological (intimate partner abuse and trauma).

It is easy to suggest that black people are in charge of South Africa and must "stop acting like victims." But this only shows a tragic disregard for the intersection of visible and invisible ways in which racism continues to afflict people. These experiences are routinely written off as anecdotes.

Jamaican psychiatrist Frederick Hickling argues that even in countries

> *where blacks are in the majority and are in political control of the society, the tangible elements of the racist delusional system still control the reality for black people.*

These elements link individual perpetrators and victims to a visible and invisible violent structure in four important ways.

How Genocide Is Defined

The legal definition of genocide is precise and includes an element that is often hard to prove, the element of "intent". The determination as to whether a situation constitutes genocide is thus factually and legally complex and should only be made following a careful and detailed examination of the facts against relevant legislation. This examination has been carried out for the purpose of establishing State responsibility or individual criminal responsibility for the crime of genocide. This must be done by a competent international or national court of law with the jurisdiction to try such cases, after an investigation meeting appropriate due process standards. According to Article IX of the Genocide Convention, disputes related to its interpretation, application and fulfilment, including State responsibility, should be addressed to the ICJ. With regards to individual criminal responsibility, Article VI determines that persons charged with genocide shall be tried by a competent court of the State in the territory of which the act was committed or by a competent international penal tribunal whose jurisdiction is accepted by the State Parties.

To date, only a few events have been determined by competent judicial bodies to constitute genocide. At the international level,

Racism as Systemic Violence

Symbolic violence is a form of "othering", defined as

> *the process of perceiving or portraying someone or something as fundamentally different or alien.*

Sociologist Pierre Bourdieu explains how this ascribes inferiority and superiority. The case of school rules about hair is an example. Galtung argues that symbolic violence justifies and legitimises structural, psychological and physical violence.

Racism; the preference for Eurocentric knowledge and methods of producing it are key examples of symbolic violence. The second and third examples marginalise and silence indigenous voices. They lead to assimilation and self-hatred. Oppressed people internalise everything about the oppressor as superior.

> the ICTR determined the killings of Tutsi in 1994 in Rwanda to be genocide. The ICTY has determined that the events in 1995 in Srebrenica (Bosnia & Herzegovina) were genocide. The ICJ also qualified the events of Srebrenica as genocide. In other instances, charges of genocide have been brought against specific individuals, but the trial or final decision in the cases in question are still pending and therefore genocide has not yet been established. Such charges have been brought, for example, by the International Criminal Court in the case of Darfur (Sudan); and by the Extraordinary Chambers in the Courts of Cambodia. At the national level, a few domestic courts have ruled that particular events constituted genocide. When considering these cases, it is important to compare the definition of the crime of genocide in the national legal framework with the international definition.
>
> National legislative and executive authorities have sometimes characterised certain incidents or periods of violence as genocide, following processes that include political assessments alongside legal considerations. These characterisations cannot be treated as authoritative or determinative, at least beyond the States concerned.
>
> **"When to Refer to a Situation as 'Genocide'," United Nations Office on Genocide Prevention and the Responsibility Project.**

Racism as Structural, Psychological, and Physical Violence

Vusi Gumede seems to suggest that structural violence is economically driven. "Othered" people around the world continue to be over-represented in society's stigmatised institutions. This is especially true in its prisons.

This is a result of inequality, unemployment, poverty and exclusion. It is driven by criminalisation and constant surveillance. It could also be because of engagement in counter-violence defined as crime. Hickling points out that

> *without control of the commanding heights of the economy, black people are destined to eke out an existence [...] in a social reality that relegates them to an economic second class.*

Racism produces inter-generationally transmitted trauma. This can persist for decades and even centuries after the original trauma. It takes far more than talk therapy and the processing of emotions to address the internalised superiority and inferiority induced by racism.

No one is held criminally liable for the uninterrupted invisible violence of racism. Unless, of course, it manifests in some forms of psychological and interpersonal physical violence.

But black people are held legally accountable for visible counter-violence against racism.

The understanding of violence as both invisible and visible provides a framework within which "othered" people can understand that experiences of racism are socially patterned. And that it requires a holistic solution.

This might include our knowledge of dehumanisation, humiliation, silencing, alienation, exclusion, economic dispossession, shame, grief, trauma and other masked experiences. All represent multiple and simultaneous effects of racism.

It can also counter the pervasive denial about the ways in which racism is kept in place culturally, socially, economically, psychologically and physically.

This framework can contribute to dislodging not only racism's manifestations, but also its structure.

Viewpoint 2

> *"In recent years many institutions in the U.S. have attempted to recognize the wrongs done to Indigenous peoples."*

Reckoning with the History of Racism and Violence Against Native Americans

Abel R. Gomez

In this viewpoint, Abel R. Gomez explains the history of the forced removal of Native Americans from their homelands in the United States. Native Americans were forced to leave their homes and move onto reservations, and Native children were separated from their families and forced to go to boarding schools where they had no choice but to assimilate. Physical, psychological, and sexual violence were common aspects of these practices. Today, efforts are being made to acknowledge the destructive, violent actions that Native Americans were subjected to, such as the creation of Indigenous Peoples Day. However, some people argue that this is not enough, and that land should be returned to Native people. At the time this viewpoint was published, Abel R. Gomez was a PhD candidate in the department of religion at Syracuse University.

"Indigenous Peoples Day comes amid a reckoning over colonialism and calls for return of Native land," by Abel R. Gomez, The Conversation, October 12, 2020. https://theconversation.com/indigenous-peoples-day-comes-amid-a-reckoning-over-colonialism-and-calls-for-return-of-native-land-147734.

As you read, consider the following questions:

1. What are some of the policies related to Indigenous lands referenced in this viewpoint?
2. What is the purpose of Indigenous land acknowledgements that have occurred in recent years, according to Gomez?
3. Besides acknowledgement, what do Indigenous leaders also believe should be done to reckon with the legacy of racist and colonialist policies?

In many parts of what is now the United States, communities have in recent years replaced Columbus Day with Indigenous Peoples Day.

Celebrating Indigenous cultures every October is important. But in this moment when the U.S. is reckoning with legacies of racism and colonialism, many Indigenous nations call for something more—the return of ancestral lands.

Having spoken to Native Americans activists, leaders and community members in the course of my research into sacred sites protection movements, I understand that land is often the center of Indigenous life. It is not just where people live, but a site of complex relationships among humans, waters, plants, animals and spiritual beings. This is why the famous Standing Rock Sioux scholar and activist Vine Deloria Jr. wrote "American Indians hold their lands—places—as having the highest possible meaning, and all their statements are made with this reference point in mind."

Stolen Lands

In my research with California Bay Area Ohlone tribes, I have learned how land is central to identity and culture. Even in highly urbanized places like San Francisco and Oakland, Ohlone people have talked to me about how the land still holds meaning.

As a non-Indigenous Latino scholar, I have also been challenged to continually reimagine those places—and the continent as a whole—as Indigenous land. Like many people in the U.S., my education growing up taught me to think about Indigenous peoples in the past tense—looking at their history and not their contemporary experiences.

This reimagining is necessary given important U.S. policies related to Indigenous lands. Laws such as the Indian Removal Act of 1830 worked to displace tribes from their homelands into "Indian Territory" in Oklahoma. This law intended to open lands for non-Native settlers.

Such is the context of the Trail of Tears, the forced removal of the Cherokee and other tribal nations from their homelands to reservations in the 1830s.

Similar policies are found in the Allotment Act of 1887, which sought to dissolve communally held reservation lands into individual allotments. After allotments were granted, the "excess land" was sold to white settlers. Tribes lost 90 million acres as a result.

Some policies sought to take away land through less explicit means. These include the establishment of Indian boarding schools that worked to assimilate tribal youth. Native children were forcibly taken from their homes to assimilate them. Many suffered physical, sexual and psychological abuse.

Other policies like the Indian Relocation Act of 1956 worked to assimilate Native peoples by encouraging them to move to major cities.

This last policy ended up backfiring significantly. Instead of assimilating, Native peoples in urban spaces eventually joined forces to create the American Indian Movement in 1968. This intertribal political movement sought to protect tribal lands, stop police brutality and hold the U.S. government accountable to treaty agreements with tribal nations.

Beyond Acknowledgements

In recent years many institutions in the U.S. have attempted to recognize the wrongs done to Indigenous peoples. For example, some organizations, universities and businesses have issued land acknowledgments—brief statements that mention the Indigenous peoples of the land where the institution operates.

The land acknowledgment at Syracuse University, where I work, is typical of such statements:

> "The Syracuse University College of Arts and Sciences would like to acknowledge with respect the Onondaga Nation, firekeepers of the Haudenosaunee, the indigenous peoples on whose ancestral lands Syracuse University now stands."

These statements work to bring awareness to Indigenous lands and peoples. They can also be a first step toward solidarity between Native and non-Native peoples. Leaders like Corrina Gould of the Bay Area's Confederated Villages of Lisjan/Ohlone encourage institutions to take this further. "Land acknowledgment must begin with a relationship with the people on whose land you are on," she said at a workshop in San Francisco. "And I think the next step I'm looking for is, how do we now live in reciprocity with one another on our homelands?"

Indigenous leaders also call for the return of land. The social media hashtag campaign #LandBack addresses this directly. *Forbes* writer Michela Moscufo traces the origins of the campaign to Indigenous activists' critique of the ways Canadian Prime Minister Justin Trudeau has handled pipelines through First Nations territories. Moscufo also notes that the phase "Land Back" has been used in the U.S. as well.

This has included protests by Lakota peoples and allies during President Trump's visit to Mount Rushmore on July 4. Mount Rushmore is part of the Black Hills, a sacred place to the Lakota that was taken by U.S. forces after gold was discovered in 1874, a violation of the 1868 Treaty of Fort Laramie.

Resistance at the U.S./Mexico Border

The phrase "Land Back" has also been invoked in resistance to the construction of the border wall between the U.S. and Mexico. Tribal nations whose territories exist along this border such as the Kumeyaay in California, Tohono O'odham in Arizona, and others are active in protesting against its construction.

Last month, two Kumeyaay activists were arrested while protesting the wall construction. The *San Diego Tribune* reported that activists were part of "Camp Land Back," which began in August to protest the wall. Kumeyaay leaders have voiced concerns that the construction of the wall will disrupt ancestral lands, especially sacred and burial sites. On the Instagram page @kumeyaaydefenseagainstthewall, the campaign describes itself as a "Small indigenous initiative that is rooted in prayer to defend Kumeyaay lands and people."

Expanding Indigenous Peoples Day

The Yellowhead Institute, a Canadian First Nations-led research center, describes "land back" as being about "reclaiming Indigenous jurisdiction" and "breathing life into rights and responsibilities."

As Indigenous peoples the world over continue to defend ancestral lands, Indigenous Peoples Day can have important meaning, more than just the renaming of a national holiday. It is an invitation to contend with the impacts of colonialism and the wrongful appropriation of Indigenous lands.

Viewpoint 3

> *"News outlets today often refer to the Tulsa race riot as a massacre. The Tulsa Historical Society and Museum calls it the 1921 Tulsa Race Massacre."*

The 1921 Tulsa Race Massacre

Clark Merrefield

In the following viewpoint Clark Merrefield outlines the history of the 1921 race massacre in Tulsa, Oklahoma. In the viewpoint, Merrefield cites historical and modern scholarship about the massacre and the many disastrous effects of the violence. Step by step, Merrefield examines the causes of this massacre, along with the multi-generational negative consequences of the tragedy. In particular, Merrefield considers the lasting financial impacts the massacre had on Black Tulsans. While it is not possible to undo the damage that was done, in the past decade there have been more attempts to reckon with the attack. Clark Merrefield is a senior editor of economics at the Harvard Kennedy School.

As you read, consider the following questions:

1. According to the viewpoint, what was Black Wall Street?
2. What caused the Tulsa Race Massacre, as reported by Merrefield?

"The 1921 Tulsa Race Massacre and the financial fallout," by Clark Merrefield, The Harvard Gazette, June 18, 2020. Reprinted by permission.

3. How did entrepreneurship and invention suffer because of the massacre, as stated by the author?

People have already lined up outside the Bank of Oklahoma (BOK) Center in Tulsa, Okla., where President Donald Trump plans to hold a rally on Saturday. The arena holds nearly 20,000 people and a nearby convention center has been reserved for overflow. Also nearby: the Greenwood District, where in 1921 a white mob numbering in the thousands destroyed an affluent Black community known as Black Wall Street.

Trump's rally comes at the moment a sudden civil rights movement has surged across the U.S. following the killing of George Floyd while in Minneapolis police custody. Amid a national swirl of racial reckoning—and the coronavirus pandemic—the rally is a go in a city still grappling with its past.

Trump moved the day of the rally from Friday to Saturday after he learned about Juneteenth, a yearly commemoration held on June 19 to observe and celebrate the end of slavery in the U.S. Numerous prominent Black leaders had called on Trump to move the date, and Gov. Kevin Stitt has recommended that Trump avoid Greenwood.

Academics describe Greenwood in 1921 as an affluent Black community of more than 10,000 residents where leaders nurtured entrepreneurship and innovation. White Tulsans deeply resented the success of their Black neighbors. On May 31, a spark set off that kindling. News reports published that day claimed a Black man, Dick Rowland, had assaulted a white woman, Sarah Page, in an elevator the day prior.

Further research suggests otherwise.

"It is commonly understood today that Rowland simply slipped and inadvertently grabbed Page's hand, prompting her to scream," write the authors of "The Destruction of Black Wall Street: Tulsa's 1921 Riot and the Eradication of Accumulated Wealth," published October 2018 in *The American Journal of Economics and Sociology*, one of the papers highlighted below.

After the elevator, white Tulsa erupted. The evening of May 31, a mob of hundreds of white Tulsans gathered at the courthouse where Rowland was being held, according to a 2001 report the Oklahoma government commissioned in part to detail the facts of the riot. Three white men from the mob went into the courthouse and demanded that officials hand over Rowland, but authorities refused, according to the report.

Rebuffed, white Tulsa invaded Black Tulsa, looting, dropping bombs from planes, and committing arson and murder over the next 12 hours. The white mob swelled into the thousands. One witness said he saw Tulsa police officers burning down Black homes. Some ten thousand Black Tulsans lost their shelter and livelihoods, and hundreds lost their lives by the time martial law was finally declared the morning of June 1.

"With estimates of from 150 to 300 dead, it was at best shameful, at worse, a massacre," writes then-Oklahoma State Sen. Maxine Horner in the state report. Indeed, news outlets today often refer to the Tulsa race riot as a massacre. The Tulsa Historical Society and Museum calls it the 1921 Tulsa Race Massacre.

Losses were devastating for Greenwood, but there's little peer-reviewed academic research on the specific economic consequences of the massacre. The three articles featured below are among the few that attempt to analyze some of the economic fallout. They estimate direct property damage from the massacre north of $200 million in today's dollars; they associate the massacre with stifling Black innovation; and they show that challenges persist when it comes to reconciling the past with the economic imperatives of today.

The economic devastation in Greenwood was essentially total and the neighborhood never recovered its status as America's Black Wall Street, according to Chris Messer, Thomas Shriver, and Alison Adams.

Messer is an associate psychology professor at Colorado State University-Pueblo. Shriver is a sociology professor at North Carolina State University. Adams is an assistant professor of community and environmental sociology at the University of Florida. They reconstruct the story of financial loss for Black entrepreneurs and families in Greenwood through archival documents, U.S. Census Bureau data, oral narratives from residents and contemporaneous news coverage.

Many Greenwood residents kept cash in their homes, in part because they didn't trust white-owned banks, according to the authors. White mobs stole money and valuables from Black households. The mobs destroyed more than 1,200 homes across 35 city blocks, and another 314 homes were looted. Some Black families from Greenwood became American refugees in America, living in Red Cross tents. Police and National Guard units imprisoned other Black residents. Others fled Tulsa. In a matter of hours, white looters had eradicated Black wealth in Greenwood.

"From a 10-room and basement modern brick home, I am now living in what was my coal barn," recalled resident C.L. Netherland, according to a contemporaneous testimonial relayed in the paper. "From a five-chair white enamel barber shop, four baths, electric clippers, electric fan, two lavatories and shampoo stands, four workmen, double marble shine stand, a porter and income of over $500 or $600 per month, to a razor, strop and folding chair on the sidewalk."

The authors estimate white rioters decimated more than $200 million of Black property in today's dollars. Courts decided the city of Tulsa was not financially liable for what the mob had done, according to the authors. Insurance companies got around claims through clauses that released them from damage payouts due to riots. The U.S. Supreme Court in 2005 decided not to hear a case seeking reparations for survivors and descendants of the Tulsa massacre, after lower courts ruled the statute of limitations had expired.

"The failure to provide reparations did not simply affect the direct victims of collective white violence," the authors write. "It was a part of a larger pattern that deprived later generations of African Americans of household assets and conveyed an implicit message that white violence would be either condoned or tolerated. That is the legacy that now demands a response."

Black inventors obtained some 726 patents from 1870 to 1940. But lynchings and other race-based violence suppressed another 1,100 patents from Black inventors during that period, finds Michigan State University economist Lisa Cook.

Cook tallied 38 riots, including the 1921 Tulsa massacre, that led to major loss of life and property. Most of the time, but not always, rioters were white people targeting Black people and their property. There were many small riots, but those incidents weren't well documented at the time the paper was published. Major riots happened mostly in the South before 1900 and in the North after 1900, Cook finds.

"The effects of violence on Black economic activity would have been both direct — for example, Black inventors' workshops were located in the affected business districts—and indirect—for example, riots lower the value of commercial and residential property, which would reduce financing opportunities and increase operating costs," Cook writes.

She also tallied 290 state laws that promoted segregation and decreased access to patenting institutions and networks of all-white patent attorneys, as well as 2,787 lynchings of Black victims and 290 lynchings of white victims during the period studied.

"In addition to killing the victim, often a secondary objective was the externality a lynching produced—to intimidate the victim's family, community, or ethnic or racial group," Cook writes. "A lynching signaled that personal security—and with it the freedom to work and innovate—was not guaranteed."

Patent records don't capture inventors' race. To fill the gaps, Cook used historical directories of Black doctors, scientists and engineers—professionals likely to be inventors—combined with U.S. Census Bureau data and U.S. Patent Office survey data. Cook documents a variety of innovations across industries by Black inventors. Judy W. Reed patented a dough kneader and roller in 1884. Alexander Miles was granted a patent for automatic elevator doors in 1887. Oscar Robert Cassell patented a flying machine in 1914. Richard E.S. Toomey got a patent in 1930 for an appliance to prevent ice on airplanes.

Before 1900, Cook finds patenting rates were lower for Black inventors than white inventors, but followed similar patterns—increasing during economic booms, decreasing during downturns. The patent rate for Black inventors drops precipitously and mostly flattens post-1900—four years after the Supreme Court's *Plessy v. Ferguson* decision legalized racial segregation. The gap between white and Black patenting rates was widest in years when racial violence was particularly high, like 1889 and 1909.

Another watershed: 1921.

"According to the historical literature, before 1921 potential victims implicitly believed that, if implored, the federal government would act," Cook writes. "The response to the Tulsa riot was considered a major policy shift in favor of nonintervention by federal and state governments. Accounts of the Tulsa riot suggest that many at the time believed that government failed at all levels, that this was a turning point in federal policy and national practice related to property-rights protection, and that the country was likely headed toward racial warfare."

After 1921, a 1 percent increase in lynchings per capita is associated with nearly the same percentage decrease in the rate of Black patent activity, Cook finds, while major riots are associated with 14 percent lower rates of Black patents. She finds no correlation between the 1921 federal policy shift and white patenting rates.

In 2013, Tulsa renamed Brady Street in its downtown arts district to M.B. Brady Street. The street had been named for Wyatt Tate Brady, a onetime Ku Klux Klan leader and city founder linked to stoking racial animosity that precipitated the 1921 massacre and who guarded his namesake hotel during the riots. Mathew Brady was a renowned Civil War photographer without ties to Tulsa. The city also gave the street an honorary name—Reconciliation Way.

City officials framed the subtle name change as a compromise between activists and business owners, according to Jordan Brasher,

Derek Alderman and Aswin Subanthore. Brasher is an assistant professor of geography at Columbus State University. Alderman is a professor of geography at the University of Tennessee-Knoxville. Subanthore was a lecturer at The George Washington University but has left academia.

The name change compromise represents "a political technology used to justify sanitizing controversial histories and prioritizing capital accumulation over social justice," the authors write. In other words, the compromise was meant to avoid disrupting the flow of business on the street, not to confront Tulsa's past, according to the authors. The sentiment is echoed in a 2012 city plan for the arts district the authors cite:

"Today, there is a faction of Tulsans who take issue with some of the associations and choices that Tate Brady was involved with, but there is no denying that he was a huge supporter of Tulsa and played a very big part in its early development."

As of July 1, 2019, the street was officially renamed Reconciliation Way, losing Brady altogether. But the yearslong debate among officials and residents over the name of a single street in a single American city reveals how a single, explosive event a century ago can leave lasting cultural and economic scars.

"Recovering, taking responsibility for, and healing the wounds of painful, racialized historical legacies has proven to be difficult and contested memory-work in the U.S. and other nations, especially in the face of resurging white nationalism and supremacy," the authors write.

Viewpoint 4

> *"We can't separate these spasms of violence from our often racially framed criminal justice system or our social practice—even though we have declared it illegal—of physical, educational and economic segregation."*

America Has Not Done Enough to Atone for Racism and Mass Violence

The Los Angeles Times Editorial Board

As this viewpoint from the Los Angeles Times *editorial board explains, the Tulsa race massacre of 1921 was a shocking and shameful moment in which America's culture of white supremacy exploded in violence. However, it is far from the only instance of racial violence in America. Attacks on Black communities in New York City in 1863, Chinese communities in Los Angeles in 1871, and countless massacres of Native Americans are among the many other examples. Furthermore, the U.S.'s history of slavery and the forced removal of Native Americans suggest this racialized violence has a basis in policy as well. As this viewpoint explains, it is important to remember that racial violence is not just a part of America's past, but its present as well. The* Los Angeles Times *is a daily newspaper that publishes news from Southern California and around the world.*

"Editorial: A century after the Tulsa massacre, we have yet to atone for America's racism," Los Angeles Times, May 31, 2021. Reprinted by permission.

As you read, consider the following questions:

1. According to this viewpoint, why have the most overt instances of white supremacy been targeted at Black Americans?
2. As stated by the authors, what is the purpose of racialized violence?
3. According to the authors, why is it important for white Americans today to acknowledge and address the legacy of racism?

If you look at the long history of white violence against Black and other nonwhite people in the United States, the rampage through the Greenwood district of Tulsa, Okla., 100 years ago today stands out for its brutality. A chance encounter between a young Black man and a young white woman operating the elevator in a four-story building led to a charge of rape; as rumors whirled and a local newspaper fanned passions, a confrontation outside the courthouse spiraled within hours into a mass attack by a white mob on the segregated Black community.

More than 300 people, nearly all of them Black, were killed as the mob looted and burned 35 square blocks of mostly Black-owned homes and businesses—Black Wall Street, it was called. Incredibly, some 5,000 Black people also were rounded up and held en masse at an outdoor sports field in "protective" detention for weeks, many not being released unless a white Tulsan vouched for them.

The scope of the violence, the damage and the deaths in Tulsa stand as a singular moment of national embarrassment, of a radically extreme display of white supremacy. But in truth it was just one of countless spasms of hate. It is of a piece with our founding practice of race-based slavery; with the 1863 riots (most infamously in New York City) in which newly draft-eligible white men rampaged through Black communities; with thousands of lynchings that were, in effect, mob attacks by white perpetrators against individual Black victims—Tulsa writ small; and with the ongoing deplorable levels of police killing often-unarmed Black Americans such as George Floyd just over a year ago.

Because slavery drove the young United States' economy —from the cotton and other farm fields of the Deep South to the Wall Street firms and other banks that financed them to the New England textile mills that bought the cotton to the seagoing merchants on the East Coast who trafficked in human chattel—our most overt displays of white supremacy historically have targeted Africans and African descendants.

And it hasn't just been violence for violence's sake. It was to send a clear and brutal message: Stay in your place, don't aspire, don't think you are the equal of white people. It was, in fact, white society saying: "We not only don't see you as equals, but we won't let you build anything of your own, either. You can't have a Black Wall Street. You can't have intergenerational wealth. That is reserved for us."

Of course, Black Americans are by no means the nation's only victims of white violence. Here in Los Angeles, a white mob descended on Chinatown in 1871 after a shootout between two rival Chinese groups that killed a white saloon owner and wounded a police officer; the mob lynched 18 Chinese people, only one of whom may have been involved in the original gunfight.

Countless Native Americans were slaughtered in sporadic massacres, often by U.S. soldiers, during the westward expansion under Manifest Destiny, a conceit framed by the notion that white America was superior to the Native people and thus divinely endowed to control the continent. That contributed to the deaths of thousands of Indigenous people in California during an extended campaign around the time of statehood to rid the region of them —a genocide.

There's too much history here to ignore, and too many atrocities to single out which groups of victims suffered the most. Black people were enslaved by the hundreds of thousands; so, to a lesser extent, were Indigenous people and Latinos. All felt the sting of white supremacy, of white rage, of white people committing violence with impunity and, at times, as an extension of government policy forged, needless to say, by white political leaders elected primarily by white men from the nation's formation through the early 20th century.

It's telling that no one can say with certainty how many Black Americans died in 1898 when white people staged a coup in Wilmington, N.C., to end a racially integrated city government (burning down a Black newspaper office in the bargain), and in 1923 when a white mob destroyed the Black Florida village of Rosewood. The killers didn't bother to keep track of the killed, although the total was easily in the dozens. And these episodes reverberate not because they were outliers but because they were part of a historical pattern.

We can't separate these spasms of violence from our often racially framed criminal justice system or our social practice—even though we have declared it illegal—of physical, educational and economic segregation. As a nation we must confront and reckon with that past and its contemporary effects.

White Americans in particular need to move beyond the rationalization that white people today did not kill Black people a century ago. Of course they didn't. But today's white Americans benefit from that legacy of racism in a society in which Black Americans have less access to healthcare, face more hurdles in accumulating wealth and accessing capital, often are educated in de facto segregated schools, and face harsher police scrutiny and more severe criminal penalties.

On the 100th anniversary of that murderous attack in Tulsa, it's important to reflect on the past, of course, and to remember the victims. Perhaps more important, though, we should not think of Tulsa—and Rosewood and Wilmington and all the other violent expressions of white supremacy—as relics of bygone eras and beliefs.

Racism still lives with us. It may not manifest itself as a mob descending on and slaughtering a Black community, or in the lynching of residents of Chinatown, or in the genocide of Native Americans. But it is still here. We must confront it, defuse it and dismantle its living legacy.

VIEWPOINT 5

The U.S. Has a Long History of Racial Massacres

Ovunc Kutlu

In this viewpoint, Ovunc Kutlu argues that although the U.S. is quick to condemn other countries for committing genocides and mass violence in other countries, the U.S. has its own extensive history of this kind of violence. This history begins with the conquest of the Americas in 1492 and the eradication of Indigenous groups that soon followed. The viewpoint considers the treatment of Native Americans and Black Americans, as well as mass killings in wars and conflicts the U.S. has fought in other countries. This includes America's use of the atomic bomb in Japan during World War II (1945), which systemically killed large numbers of Japanese people, as well as the many deaths that have occurred in the wars in Vietnam, Iraq, and Afghanistan. Ovunc Kutlu is a correspondent for Anadolu Agency, a state-run news agency in Turkey.

As you read, consider the following questions:

1. According to data cited in this viewpoint, how many Indigenous people in the Western Hemisphere are estimated to have been killed or died prematurely because of Europeans and people of European descent?
2. What are examples of racial violence in early U.S. wars that are listed in this viewpoint?

"US history riddled with massacres, genocide," by Ovunc Kutlu, Anadolu Agency, June 2, 2021. Reprinted by permission.

3. Approximately how many people were killed in Nagasaki and Hiroshima, Japan, when the U.S. dropped atomic bombs on these cities?

History records US genocide against Native Americans, Africans, massacres in Southeast Asia, Middle East.

Ankara

US President Joe Biden's controversial recognition of 1915 events between Armenians and Turks as genocide brings to light massacres in American history in the last 500 years.

Biden called the events of 1915 an "Armenian genocide" on April 24, breaking American presidents' long-held tradition of refraining from using the term.

But during the course of American history, the US and its European ancestors have been involved in numerous massacres and carried out genocides against indigenous peoples.

Genocide is an act committed with intent to destroy, in whole or in part, a national, ethnic, racial or religious group, according to the Geneva Convention.

With that in mind, the conquest of the Americas in 1492, European colonization led to the systematic eradication of indigenous peoples on the continent.

Native American Genocide

The 13 American colonies' population grew from about 2,000 to 2.4 million between 1625 and 1775 while displacing Native Americans from eastern North America.

After the colonies declared independence in 1776 from Great Britain and formed the US, the settlers started to move west, clashing with and eradicating the Apache, Cherokee, Cheyenne, Chinook, Navajo and Sioux tribes. Some of the names today are sadly used for American warfare helicopters and ubiquitous sport utility vehicles.

The national holiday, Thanksgiving, celebrated in November, is traced to the 1620s when European settlers invited Native Americans to a feast. The settlers later killed the population and gave thanks to God for allowing them to slaughter the "savages."

The surviving descendants of Native American tribes live in poverty on federally recognized Indian reservations across the US.

Almost 100 million indigenous people in the Western Hemisphere have been killed or died prematurely because of the Europeans and their descendants in five centuries, according to David E. Stannard in his book, *American Holocaust: The Conquest of the New World*.

Around 12 million indigenous people died within present US geographical boundaries between 1492 and 1900, according to Russell Thornton in *American Indian Holocaust and Survival: A Population History Since 1492*.

Genocides Against Africans and Slavery

Despite having unalienable rights—life, liberty and the pursuit of happiness—as enshrined in the American Declaration of Independence, not all in the new colonies were considered equal.

The colonies had a system of slavery, which European settlers carried as a practice into the Americas from the Old World, despite English Protestants praising themselves as Puritans.

A conservative estimate of 35 million men, women and children were brought from Africa to the New World between the 16th and 19th centuries.

Around 12.5 million of those brought to North America were used as free labor in fields and worked under grueling conditions, according to the Trans-Atlantic Slave Trade Database.

The systematic repression of Africans continues to the present day in the US government application of laws, health and education.

Early US Wars

A century before gaining civil rights and liberties, Blacks had to fight in the white man's wars in the US military.

More than 200,000 Blacks joined Union forces in the American Civil War, while an unaccounted number of free and slave Blacks were used for manual labor in the Confederacy. The war that began in 1861 and lasted until 1865 left 750,000 soldiers dead with an undetermined number of civilians.

Despite overthrowing its colonial ruler, Great Britain, the US pursued colonial interests in Southeast Asia during the late 19th century.

Around 20,000 Filipino combatants and as many as 200,000 civilians died from violence, famine, and disease during the Philippine–American War between 1899-1902, according to the State Department's Office of the Historian.

On the domestic front in the early 20th century, the Tulsa race massacre in 1921 saw white residents attacking the Black population and burning their businesses and homes.

Almost 300 Black people were killed as a result, and more than 800 were injured in the massacre that left over 10,000 Black people homeless.

Biden said Tuesday it was no riot, but instead a hate-fueled "massacre," adding "As soon as it happened there was a clear effort to erase it from our collective memory, from the news and everyday conversations."

Atomic Bomb and Cold War Coups

The US, along with allies in the UK and France, won World War II with the Soviet Union against Nazi Germany. But it was the end of the war that marked the American massacre against Imperial Japan in the Pacific and the advent of the atomic bomb.

Japanese casualties were around 110,000 in the battle for Okinawa, the largest and bloodiest battle of the war.

To end it all, the US dropped two atomic bombs on Japan in 1945 that killed an estimated 140,000 people in Hiroshima and 74,000 in Nagasaki, according to the global civil society coalition International Campaign to Abolish Nuclear Weapons.

The US emerged as one of two remaining superpowers in global politics after the war and extended its scope to South America, Middle East, Western Europe and Far Asia.

The first proxy war in the Cold War era came in Korea from 1950-53, with more than 930,000 Koreans and Chinese forces dead. On the civilian side, more than 1,550,000 North Koreans died, while 990,000 South Koreans were killed, bringing the death toll to nearly 3.5 million.

To exert control on Iranian oil resources, the US and the UK orchestrated an Iranian coup in 1953 to overthrow democratically elected Prime Minister Mohammad Mosaddegh and strengthened the monarchical rule of Shah Mohammad Reza Pahlavi. The coup killed 300, while an estimated 10,000 were executed in years to follow.

The US treated Central and South American countries as its backyard during the Cold War to steer governments away from socialism and communism.

A Guatemalan coup in 1954 deposed democratically-elected Guatemalan President Jacobo Arbenz with the support of the US and installed the military dictatorship of Carlos Castillo Armas. Guatemala fell into a civil war for the next three decades, with 200,000 people killed.

The 1973 Chilean coup that deposed the Popular Unity government of President Salvador Allende saw Gen. Augusto Pinochet seize power with the support of the US. A truth and reconciliation report in 1991 found that more than 2,000 were killed.

The US sold more than $120 million in military equipment to Argentina in 1977 and 1978 alone as part of Operation Condor, which caused an estimated death toll of at least 60,000 people.

Vietnam War

Arguably the deadliest war in US history came in Vietnam when Washington wanted to contain the spread of communism in Southeast Asia, but the conflict lasted two decades, which also spilled into Cambodia and Laos.

The number of Vietnamese civilians dead is estimated as high as 2 million, with another 1.8 million killed during the fighting. About 18.2 million gallons of Agent Orange was sprayed from American fighter planes from 1961 to 1971. The Vietnamese government claimed 400,000 people were killed from the chemical and 500,000 children were born with congenital disabilities.

While the Cambodian Civil War killed 300,000, the Laotian Civil War caused more than 60,000 dead. That brought the massacre's toll to almost 4.2 million.

Iraq, Afghanistan

After Asia, the US turned its attention to the Middle East from the 1990s with the Gulf War. Washington's presence in the region intensified in the aftermath of the Sept. 11 terror attacks in the US and changed the whole landscape in the Middle East.

The Gulf War caused around 5,000 civilian deaths, but it was the subsequent wars that saw casualties rise exponentially.

From the beginning of the US invasion of Iraq in 2003, through its insurgency and civil war, more than 1 million are estimated to have been killed.

Around 240,000 have died in the US war zone in Afghanistan and Pakistan since 2001.

As of April 2021, more than 71,000 Afghan and Pakistani civilians are estimated to have lost their lives as a direct result of the war, according to Brown University.

Periodical and Internet Sources Bibliography

The following articles have been selected to supplement the diverse views presented in this chapter.

Sarah Fling, "The Formerly Enslaved Households of President Andrew Johnson," the White House Historical Association, March 5, 2020. https://www.whitehousehistory.org/the-formerly-enslaved-households-of-president-andrew-johnson.

Hassan Kanu, "U.S. Confronts 'Cultural Genocide in Native American Boarding School Probe," Reuters, May 18, 2022. https://www.reuters.com/legal/government/us-confronts-cultural-genocide-native-american-boarding-school-probe-2022-05-18/.

Alysa Landry, "Presidents and Native Peoples," *Cowboys & Indians*, June 18, 2020. https://www.cowboysindians.com/2020/06/presidents-and-native-peoples/.

Robert S. Levine, "On the Racism of Andrew Johnson, Self-Identified White Ally and 'Your Moses,'" *Literary Hub*, August 24, 2021. https://lithub.com/on-the-racism-of-andrew-johnson-self-identified-white-ally-and-your-moses/.

Yun Li, "Black Wall Street Was Shattered 100 Years Ago. How the Tulsa Race Massacre Was Covered Up and Unearthed," CNBC, May 31, 2021. https://www.npr.org/2022/12/11/1137090651/elaine-massacre-tulsa-race-riot.

Scott Neuman, "In Two U.S. Cities Haunted by Race Massacres, Facing the Past is Painful and Divisive," NPR, December 11, 2022. https://www.npr.org/2022/12/11/1137090651/elaine-massacre-tulsa-race-riot.

Yuliya Parshina-Kottas, "What the Tulsa Race Massacre Destroyed," *New York Times*, May 24, 2021. https://www.nytimes.com/interactive/2021/05/24/us/tulsa-race-massacre.html.

David Priess, "How a Difficult, Racist, Stubborn President Was Removed from Power—If Not from Office," *Politico*, November 13, 2018. https://lithub.com/on-the-racism-of-andrew-johnson-self-identified-white-ally-and-your-moses/.

Randi Richardson, "Tulsa Race Massacre, 100 Years Later: Why It Happened and Why It's Still Relevant Today," NBC News, May

28, 2021. https://www.nbcnews.com/news/nbcblk/tulsa-race-massacre-100-years-later-why-it-happened-why-n1268877.

Ron Rosenbaum, "The Shocking Savagery of America's Early History," *Smithsonian Magazine*, March 2013. https://www.smithsonianmag.com/history/the-shocking-savagery-of-americas-early-history-22739301/.

OPPOSING VIEWPOINTS® SERIES

Chapter 3

Where Do Genocides Happen, and Why Do They Happen?

Chapter Preface

Genocide has happened in the past, and mass atrocities continue to happen today. Some areas around the world may seem to be especially prone to extreme violence, but the authors in this chapter's viewpoints suggest that no country is immune to genocide. This raises the questions: Could genocide happen in a stable democracy? Could it happen in the United States?

In certain instances of genocide, one can point a finger at the type of governing body that controls a country and assume this to be a major cause of genocidal violence. Countries that are politically unstable—such as those with large amounts of political upheaval, economic turmoil, and war—have been responsible for genocides in the past and are proving to be capable of the same violence in the present. The viewpoints in this chapter also examine certain behaviors that have been characterized as warning signs for genocide and other forms of mass violence—such as dehumanization, polarization, and classification that leads to "othering"—and consider examples of how these behaviors have played out in particular countries. Some of the authors in this chapter also consider whether these behaviors have happened or are currently happening in the United States.

This chapter's viewpoints explore where genocides have happened and why. Expert authors provide the reader with analysis on how genocides have happened in Cambodia, Rwanda, and Bosnia. A more recent viewpoint quotes U.S. President Joe Biden as saying that he believes Russia's invasion of Ukraine is a genocide occurring today. Many of the viewpoints in this chapter cover the topic of dehumanization and how this practice is a root cause of mass violence and genocide. Interestingly, experts explain that the tendency to commit dehumanization is psychological, and they provide examples of this happening today in democracies—the United States for one.

Viewpoint 1

"This past week, President Biden again ratcheted up his rhetoric when he told an audience in Iowa President Vladimir Putin was 'a dictator [who] commits genocide.'"

President Biden Accuses Vladimir Putin of Committing Genocide in Ukraine

Ron Elving

In the following viewpoint, Ron Elving argues that Russian President Vladimir Putin is waging a genocide in Ukraine. Ron Elving cites evidence gathered by the U.S. and Ukraine providing historical background about the recognition of genocide and argues that the Biden administration has made a point of recognizing more acts of atrocities as genocides than past administrations. Elving describes how some instances of atrocities are designated as genocides, and finally cites a list of the genocides that have occurred around the world to help clarify how genocides occur, what characteristics they possess, and how they are punished. Ron Elving is a senior editor and correspondent at the Washington desk for NPR.

As you read, consider the following questions:

1. According to this viewpoint, why is it ironic that the word "genocide" is being used to describe the Russian invasion of Ukraine?
2. Which U.S. government agency is responsible for deciding which mass killings are genocide, according to the author?
3. How many genocides have taken place since the Holocaust, according to Secretary of State Antony Blinken?

Cities are being bombed, warships sunk and tens of thousands of soldiers and civilians have been killed. And as the real struggle in Ukraine continues to intensify, so does the accompanying war of words.

This past week, President Biden again ratcheted up his rhetoric when he told an audience in Iowa President Vladimir Putin was "a dictator [who] commits genocide."

In remarks made after Putin's armed forces invaded Ukraine in February, Biden had called the atrocities reported from that country "war crimes." He had called Putin a "war criminal" who said he needed to be removed from power. (The White House subsequently walked back the latter comment.) Nonetheless, his use of the word genocide detonated in the media and spread shock waves through the international community.

Many observers have suggested that if Ukraine is right about the systematic murder of its civilians, these acts fit the definition of "war crimes" or "crimes against humanity" as understood by international courts for generations. Deliberate targeting of civilians is definitionally a war crime.

But Biden went further: "Yes, I called it genocide. It has become clearer and clearer that Putin is just trying to wipe out the idea of even being—being able to be Ukrainian."

Each presidential turn of the rhetorical ratchet in recent weeks has made news, catching NATO allies off guard and prompting "clarification" from the White House. Yet each has also set a tone for much of the war debate that followed.

It should also be noted that in each instance of provocative language Biden has been essentially following the lead of his Ukrainian counterpart, Volodymyr Zelenskyy. The Ukrainian president has also personalized the struggle, calling Putin out for war crimes and labeling the killing of civilians in Ukraine as genocide.

Most recently, Zelenskyy has called on the U.S. to add Russia to its list of "state sponsors of terrorism," which now includes the regimes in Syria, Iran, Cuba and North Korea.

That list, too, is often misunderstood and subject to interpretation, but it was begun in 1979 and used by subsequent presidents in both parties to justify various acts against several countries—including Iraq, Sudan, Libya and South Yemen.

Appropriating Putin's Own Language

There is a degree of irony in the use of the word "genocide" at this stage of the war because it figured so prominently in Putin's own rhetoric prior to the invasion. In February, Putin accused Ukrainian forces of killing Russian-speaking separatists in the eastern part of the country (known as the Donbas for its geographic role as the basin of the Don River).

"What is happening in the Donbas today is genocide," Putin told his country on Feb. 15. Thereafter, a chorus of other Russian voices in government and the media took up the theme. Russia even complained to the United Nations Security Council that Ukraine was "exterminating the civilian population" in the Donbas.

Putin provided no evidence for this claim at the time and has not since. But the accusation has been part of the Russian media campaign against the government in Kyiv since a popular uprising deposed a pro-Putin autocrat there in 2014. It is often invoked in discussions of Russian ethnicity and the importance of protecting culturally Russian people wherever they may live.

Still, the sudden prominence of the genocide term this past winter seemed a warning that Putin was about to make a move. And indeed, a little more than a week later, Russian tanks rolled into Ukraine—not only in the Donbas but on the highway to Kyiv.

The latter thrust was stymied well shy of its objectives by the now-famous resistance of the Ukrainian armed forces and armed civilians. But as the Russians retreated they left evidence of a massacre, widely documented by Western journalists, that included women and children and men who had been bound.

Cities and towns in Ukraine had already been pounded by Russian bombs and missiles fired indiscriminately at densely populated areas. But it was the emergence of atrocities in towns such as Bucha that caught the world's attention, spawned a fresh round of international sanctions and prompted renewed talk of war crimes and genocide.

What It Means

Genocide was a term first used in the 1940s, describing the Holocaust—Nazi Germany's effort to eradicate all the Jews in Europe and elsewhere (along with other categories of people deemed undesirable). The United Nations Genocide Convention in 1948 characterized several "acts committed with intent to destroy, in whole or in part, a national, ethnic, racial or religious people." Others have used somewhat broader categories or groupings.

Whatever differences of interpretation there may be, genocide connotes the most egregious offense imaginable in law or morality. Given the monstrous model of the Holocaust, most scholars, jurists and international leaders have preferred to use the term genocide judiciously.

"We're going to learn more and more about the devastation," Biden said. "And we'll let the lawyers decide internationally whether or not it qualifies. But it sure seems that way to me."

In the past, such determinations have taken time. There is a formal process by which the U.S. Department of State grants "recognition" of a genocide that has taken place or is taking place in some part of the world. The word recognition conveys a sense that these events are often disputed or covered up, or that they have not been widely acknowledged.

The idea that the U.S. government would make a judgment on such events is profoundly political, both in contemporary and historical terms. Since coming to office, the Biden administration has made two such recognitions—one for a genocide more than a century ago and one happening right now.

Rohingya and Armenians

Secretary of State Antony Blinken made reference to this process and the situation in Ukraine when he spoke at the U.S. Holocaust Memorial Museum in Washington, D.C., on March 22. Blinken was there to announce the completion of the recognition process with regard to Myanmar, also called Burma.

"Beyond the Holocaust, the United States has concluded that genocide was committed seven times," said Blinken. "Today marks the eighth, as I have determined that members of the Burmese military committed genocide and crimes against humanity against the Rohingya."

The Rohingya are Muslims who had lived in Burma and often been persecuted before elements of the military began trying to eliminate them entirely in 2016. Thousands have been killed and more than a million have fled the country, many to neighboring Bangladesh where they live as refugees.

But in the same speech, Blinken talked about the "unprovoked, brutal war" Russia was waging against Ukraine and "innocent men, women and children."

He noted that some of the deaths had taken place in the Kyiv area on a site known as Babyn Yar, where more than 33,000 Jews were killed by Nazis in just two days in 1941.

The case of the Rohingya was considered through the years of the Trump administration but no final decision was made. However, on his last day in office, Trump's Secretary of State Mike Pompeo did announce the recognition of genocide in another long-running and similar situation. This involved China and the systematic abuse and relocation of its Muslim Uyghurs, the largest ethnic minority group in the western Xinjiang province.

Pompeo's last-minute recognition regarding the Uyghurs was the sixth such genocide recognition made by the U.S. State Department. The seventh was added not long after, in March 2021, when a newly inaugurated President Biden ended a century-long argument about the treatment of the Armenian people by Turkey, then still known as the Ottoman Empire in 1915-16.

Although many different governments have held power in Turkey since, all have strenuously objected to calling the deaths of more than a million Armenians a genocide. Millions of dollars were spent over the years on American lobbyists, including some former members of Congress, to argue against such a recognition, largely because it was presumably damaging to U.S.-Turkish relations.

Many other mass killings throughout history have not been formally recognized by the U.S. for a variety of reasons. Some of these have been prosecuted by international courts, sometimes with U.S. support. One example is the untold loss of life in Cambodia under the Khmer Rouge regime of Pol Pot in the 1970s.

The other five genocides that have received official recognition by the U.S. since the formal process began in 1989 are noted here in the order of their official recognition.

- **Bosnia (1993)** based on the massacre of more than 8,000 Muslim men and boys in the town of Srebrenica by Serbian soldiers and militia. The killings were part of a campaign of "ethnic cleansing" conducted under Serbian leader Slobodan Milosevic and carried out largely by his army's commander Ratko Mladic.
- **Rwanda (1994)** This recognition was based on events in a civil war that had lasted for several years. In an organized campaign lasting several months, the dominant Hutu in this central African country sought to wipe out or drive out the minority ethnic Tutsi, as well as some of their own people

who tried to defend the Tutsi and a third ethnic group called the Twa. More than half a million Tutsi are believed to have been killed.

- **Iraq (1995)** The recognition came well after Ba'athist Party strongman Saddam Hussein's campaign against Iraqi Kurds began in the previous decade and lasted into the new century. Saddam at one point used poison gas against a Kurdish city named Halabja in northern Iraq. Captured after the Second Persian Gulf War, he was executed in 2006 while still on trial for earlier crimes against the Kurds.
- **Darfur (2004)** A civil war in the western parts of Sudan pitted two rebel groups against the government in Khartoum. The government armed militias, including the Janjaweed, to counter the rebellion. The United Nations estimated this resulted in the deaths of at least 200,000 and the displacement of more than two million. The leader of Janjaweed went on trial before the International Court in the Hague this spring.
- **ISIS occupied territories (2016-2017)** Yazidi, Kurds and some Christians who lived in parts of Iraq, Syria, Egypt and Libya held by the Islamic State in the second decade of this century were the victims of systematic attacks and efforts to eliminate them.

Viewpoint 2

> *"Dehumanization has the function of decommissioning our moral sentiments. In dehumanizing others, we exclude them from the circle of moral obligation. We can then kill, oppress, and enslave them with impunity."*

Dehumanization Precedes Genocide

David Livingstone Smith

In the following viewpoint, David Livingstone Smith maintains that human beings easily commit the act of dehumanization against one another. Smith examines the roots behind the act of dehumanization, including the thought processes that enable the behavior and the role it plays in marginalizing groups of people and committing acts of violence against them. He then cites evidence of dehumanization from history. He also argues that Western countries are equally guilty of dehumanization, particularly towards perpetrators and victims of genocides. David Livingstone Smith is a professor of philosophy at the University of New England in Australia, and the author of eight books on various philosophical social issues.

As you read, consider the following questions:

1. What is essentialism, as explained in this viewpoint?

"Dehumanization, Genocide, and the Psychology of Indifference," by David Livingstone Smith, Psychology Today LLC, December 2, 2011. Reprinted by permission.

2. What two factors work together in a person's belief system to allow them to dehumanize a person, according to the author?
3. What is a historical event when a group of people dehumanized another group of individuals cited in this viewpoint?

We human beings have a remarkable ability to dehumanize one another: to conceive of others as subhuman creatures, and to treat them accordingly.

I argue in my book *Less Than Human: Why We Demean, Enslave, and Exterminate Other*s (St. Martin's Press, 2011) that there are two powerful psychological forces that fuel the dehumanizing impulse. One is psychological essentialism. Psychological essentialism is the tendency to think that every kind of living thing possesses a unique essence: a mysterious inner quality that makes it a member of that kind. Consider dogs. Dogs come in an enormous range of shapes, colors, and sizes. However, we are inclined to think that they all share a common canine essence, the possession of which makes them all dogs. Similarly, we imagine that we human beings are endowed with a special human essence (a human "soul," if you will), and that it's this that makes us human.

One important feature of essentialist thinking is the notion that the essence of a thing is distinct from its appearance. Put simply, things can seem to be something other than what they really are. This principle is crucial for understanding dehumanization, because it implies that someone can appear to be human in appearance but lack a human essence. Think of them as counterfeit human beings.

Scientifically speaking, this is nonsense. There's no such thing as a canine essence or a human essence. Nevertheless, the essentialist mindset is deeply entrenched in the human psyche and powerfully influences the ways that we make sense of the world.

The second psychological dynamic behind dehumanization is the belief that nature is arranged as a hierarchy. In earlier centuries, this was known as the Great Chain of Being. God, the most perfect being, was assigned to the topmost position in the cosmic pecking order, and inert matter was thought to lie at the bottom, with every living creature situated at some intermediate position. We humans (modest beings that we are) have always placed ourselves near the uppermost rank, and have supposed that every other creature is *less than human.*

Even though the notion of the Great Chain of Being is radically at odds with our scientific picture of the cosmos, it maintains an iron grip on the human imagination. It is very difficult for us not to conceive of the world in terms of dichotomies like "higher" and "lower," "human," and "subhuman."

These two factors—essentialism and the belief in a cosmic hierarchy—work in tandem when people dehumanize one another. The dehumanized person is imagined as a human-looking creature with a subhuman essence. They are inferior animals misleadingly dressed up as human beings. This is how European colonists conceived of Native Americans, and how slave owners conceived of their human chattel. This is how the Nazis conceived of Jews, and how Rwandan Hutus conceived of their Tutsi neighbors. This way of thinking is reflected in dehumanizing epithets-referring to whole populations as lice, flies, rats, bacilli, dogs, wolves, monsters, and so on.

Dehumanization has the function of decommissioning our moral sentiments. In dehumanizing others, we exclude them from the circle of moral obligation. We can then kill, oppress, and enslave them with impunity. Taking the life of a dehumanized person becomes of no greater consequence than crushing an insect under one's boot. Here is a case in point. *Right now, as you read these words, genocidal violence is gathering momentum in Sudan.* The government of Omar Hassan Ahmad Al-Bashir, a man who has been charged by the International Criminal Court with war crimes, crimes against humanity, and genocide, is ethnically cleansing Sudan of its marginalized people. The violence is not restricted to Darfur, where between two and four hundred thousand people have already been murdered. It has spread to Abyei, the Blue Nile State, the Nuba mountains, and possibly elsewhere. It's clear from the rhetoric of the Janjaweed militias that dehumanization lubricates the machinery of slaughter in Sudan.

> "Dog, son of dogs, we came to kill you and your kids."
>
> "Kill the black donkeys! Kill the black dogs! Kill the black monkeys!"
>
> "You blacks are not human. We can do anything we want to you."
>
> "We kill our cows when they have black calves. We will kill you too."
>
> "You make this area dirty; we are here to clean the area."
>
> "You blacks are like monkeys. You are not human."

There is no disputing the fact that dehumanization and atrocity often go hand in hand. But what about indifference to atrocity? Might not dehumanization be implicated in this as well? The philosopher Richard Rorty thought so. In a paper written in 1992, when Serbian forces were engaged in the ethnic cleansing of Bosnia, Rorty argued that those of us who are safely cocooned in affluent Western democracies tend to dehumanize both the perpetrators and the victims of genocide. "We think of Serbs or Nazis as animals," he observed, "because ravenous beasts of prey are animals. We think of Muslims or Jews being herded into concentration camps as animals, because cattle are animals. Neither sort of animal is very much like us, and there seems to be no point in human beings being involved in quarrels between animals."

It is easy to recognize and condemn blatant dehumanization perpetrated by Janjaweed *genocidaires*. It is more difficult to interrogate our own indifference. Although this sort of self-examination can be deeply unsettling, there is compensation to be gained in a life that is more completely in accord with one's moral convictions, and the satisfaction of adding one more voice to the growing chorus of those who refuse to turn their backs on the people of Sudan.

Viewpoint 3

> *"Protracted conflict strains relationships and makes it difficult for parties to recognize that they are part of a shared human community."*

Dehumanization Paved the Way for Violence in Multiple Countries

Michelle Maiese

In the following viewpoint, Michelle Maiese explains the concept of dehumanization and how it leads to violence. Maiese maintains that categorizing people as "others" or being seen as outside of one's group causes various forms of irrational thinking and actions that can lead to behavior not normally accepted by most people in societies. In the final section of this viewpoint, Heidi Burgess provides an update asserting that this path of dehumanization is happening in the United States, which could lead to mass violence if left unchecked. Michelle Maiese was a graduate student at the University of Colorado at Boulder at the time this viewpoint was originally published. Heidi Burgess is founder and co-director of the University of Colorado Conflict Information Consortium.

As you read, consider the following questions:

1. As explained in this viewpoint, how does moral exclusion play a part in dehumanization?

"Dehumanization," by Michelle Maiese, University of Colorado. Originally published in July 2003, updated by Heidi Burgess in June 2020. Reprinted with permission of Beyond Intractability.

2. How are groups of people dehumanized, as stated by the author?
3. According to this viewpoint, could mass atrocities happen in the U.S. because of the trend of dehumanization?

Dehumanization is a psychological process whereby opponents view each other as less than human and thus not deserving of moral consideration. Jews in the eyes of Nazis and Tutsis in the eyes of Hutus (in the Rwandan genocide) are but two examples. Protracted conflict strains relationships and makes it difficult for parties to recognize that they are part of a shared human community. Such conditions often lead to feelings of intense hatred and alienation among conflicting parties. The more severe the conflict, the more the psychological distance between groups will widen. Eventually, this can result in moral exclusion. Those excluded are typically viewed as inferior, evil, or criminal.[1]

We typically think that all people have some basic human rights that should not be violated. Innocent people should not be murdered, raped, or tortured. Rather, international law suggests that they should be treated justly and fairly, with dignity and respect. They deserve to have their basic needs met, and to have some freedom to make autonomous decisions. In times of war, parties must take care to protect the lives of innocent civilians on the opposing side. Even those guilty of breaking the law should receive a fair trial, and should not be subject to any sort of cruel or unusual punishment.

However, for individuals viewed as outside the scope of morality and justice, "the concepts of deserving basic needs and fair treatment do not apply and can seem irrelevant."[2] Any harm that befalls such individuals seems warranted, and perhaps even morally justified. Those excluded from the scope of morality are typically perceived as psychologically distant, expendable, and deserving of treatment that would not be acceptable for those included in one's moral community. Common criteria for exclusion include ideology, skin color, and cognitive capacity. We typically dehumanize those whom we perceive as a threat to our well-being or values.[3]

Psychologically, it is necessary to categorize one's enemy as sub-human in order to legitimize increased violence or justify the violation of basic human rights. Moral exclusion reduces restraints against harming or exploiting certain groups of people. In severe cases, dehumanization makes the violation of generally-accepted norms of behavior regarding one's fellow man seem reasonable, or even necessary.

The Psychology of Dehumanization

Dehumanization is actually an extension of a less intense process of developing an "enemy image" of the opponent. During the course of protracted conflict, feelings of anger, fear, and distrust shape the way that the parties perceive each other. Adversarial attitudes and perceptions develop and parties begin to attribute negative traits to their opponent. They may come to view the opponent as an evil enemy, deficient in moral virtue, or as a dangerous, warlike monster. Such images can stem from a desire for group identity and a need to contrast the distinctive attributes and virtues of one's own group with the vices of the "outside" group.[4] In some cases, evil-ruler enemy images form. While ordinary group members are regarded as neutral, or perhaps even innocent, their leaders are viewed as hideous monsters.[5]

Enemy images are usually black and white. The negative actions of one's opponent are thought to reflect their fundamental evil nature, traits, or motives.[6] One's own faults, as well as the values and motivations behind the actions of one's opponent, are usually discounted, denied, or ignored. It becomes difficult to empathize or see where one's opponent is coming from. Meaningful communication is unlikely, and it becomes difficult to perceive any common ground.

Once formed, enemy images tend to resist change, and serve to perpetuate and intensify the conflict. Because the adversary has come to be viewed as a "diabolical enemy," the conflict is framed as a war between good and evil.[7] Once the parties have framed the conflict in this way, their positions become more rigid. In some cases, zero-sum thinking develops as parties come to believe that they must either secure their own victory, or face defeat. New goals to punish or destroy the opponent arise, and in some cases more militant leadership comes into power.

Enemy images are accentuated, according to psychologists, by the process of "projection," in which people "project" their own faults onto their opponents. This means that people or groups who tend to be aggressive or selfish are likely to attribute those traits to their opponents, but not to themselves. This improves one's own self-image and increases group cohesion, but it also escalates the conflict and makes it easier to dehumanize the other side.

Deindividuation facilitates dehumanization as well. This is the psychological process whereby a person is seen as a member of a category or group rather than as an individual. Because people who are deindividuated seem less than fully human, they are viewed as less protected by social norms against aggression than those who are individuated.[8] It then becomes easier to rationalize contentious moves or severe actions taken against one's opponents.

Dangers of Dehumanization

While deindividuation and the formation of enemy images are very common, they form a dangerous process that becomes especially damaging when it reaches the level of dehumanization.

Once certain groups are stigmatized as evil, morally inferior, and not fully human, the persecution of those groups becomes more psychologically acceptable. Restraints against aggression and violence begin to disappear. Not surprisingly, dehumanization increases the likelihood of violence and may cause a conflict to escalate out of control. Once a violence break over has occurred, it may seem even more acceptable for people to do things that they would have regarded as morally unthinkable before.

Parties may come to believe that destruction of the other side is necessary, and pursue an overwhelming victory that will cause one's opponent to simply disappear. This sort of into-the-sea framing can cause lasting damage to relationships between the conflicting parties, making it more difficult to solve their underlying problems and leading to the loss of more innocent lives.

Indeed, dehumanization often paves the way for human rights violations, war crimes, and genocide. For example, in WWII, the dehumanization of the Jews ultimately led to the destruction of millions of people.[9] Similar atrocities have occurred in Rwanda, Cambodia, and the former Yugoslavia.

It is thought that the psychological process of dehumanization might be mitigated or reversed through humanization efforts, the development of empathy, the establishment of personal relationships between conflicting parties, and the pursuit of common goals.

Current Implications

Everything in this article is still true. The only thing that is missing is an example from the United States. The examples provided in 2003 were the Holocaust, the Rwandan Genocide, Cambodia, the former Yugoslavia. In 2003, we were not thinking such a process was happening or was likely to happen in the United States.

But here we are!

Read this excerpt by Alexander Theodoridis and James Martherus in the *Washington Post*[10] from May 2018:

> *President Trump's comments during a roundtable on California's "sanctuary" law have prompted an uproar. "We have people coming into the country, or trying to come in—and we're stopping a lot of them—but we're taking people out of the country," Trump said. "You wouldn't believe how bad these people are. These aren't people. These are animals." The White House heightened this phrasing in a news release, even as pundits like E.J. Dionne pushed back on the dangers of such language.*[10]

Trump's Recitation of a Poem at Rallies Raises Concerns of Dehumanization

It's not the first time the President has read out the poem.

It featured prominently during his 2016 election campaign and has been read out on several occasions since Trump took office.

However, the true meaning of the poem appears to have been lost on the President.

To Trump, "The Snake" serves as a cautionary tale of the potential dangers posed by illegal immigrants.

The lyrics describe the story of a woman who takes a snake into her home after discovering it freezing to death outside her home.

Things take a turn for the worse, however, when after nursing the snake back to health, the serpent bites her, infecting the woman with a deadly poison in the process.

Asking the snake why he tricked her, the reptile replies that the "silly woman" knew "damn well" what it was when she took it in.

While the supposed anti-immigration message at the heart of the Trump administration, which includes a crackdown on undocumented Irish in the US – it would appear that the true meaning of the poem has been lost in translation.

"The Snake" actually started life as a song recorded by soul singer Al Wilson in 1968.

More significantly still, it was actually penned by a noted civil rights activist, Oscar Brown who wrote it as a "celebration of black culture and a repudiation of racism."

In fact, Trump has been warned by two of Brown's surviving children to stop using the song to "demonise immigrants."

Brown's family hit out at the President in a previous statement accusing him of "perversely" using the song, adding that the writer "never had anything against immigrants."

Despite issuing a cease and desist letter, Trump has continued reciting the lyrics at rallies.

"Donald Trump recites controversial poem 'The Snake' during rally," by Jack Beresford, The Irish Post, November 2, 2020.

But the article continues to explain that it isn't just President Trump, nor is it just Republicans. Reporting on a survey Theodoridis and Martherus did,

> *Seventy-seven percent of our respondents rated their political opponents as less evolved. [They asked respondents to rank members of their own and the opposing party on a scale from zero to 100. Accompanying the scale was an image of the evolution of humans, with 0 being apes and 100 being a modern human (with Neanderthal and other primitive humanoids in between.] Respondents who considered themselves strong partisans were more likely to dehumanize opposing partisans, and Republicans and Democrats were equally likely to dehumanize their opponents.* [10]

Indeed, Democrats do dehumanize Republicans, particularly Trump supporters, when they accuse them of being ignorant, hateful, or "deplorables" as was famously once said by Hillary Clinton in the last Presidential campaign. Accusing all Republicans of being racist bigots is similar, and is taken as badly by the right as the left takes Trump's attacks, as is evidenced by this blog by a Ben Armstrong, a conservative newscaster from Wisconsin.[11] The contempt with which law enforcement officers and departments are now widely viewed after the George Floyd killing (assuming all police are racists, for example) along with widespread calls that they be "defunded" (and all officers presumably fired) is coming precariously close to dehumanization as well.

As Maiese argued in the original article, such dehumanization can lead to violence. Both Theodoridis and Martherus (in the *Washington Post* study) and Ben Armstrong's blog[11] point to the shooting at the Republican Congressional baseball team:

> *...when James Hodgkinson opened fire on congressional Republicans while they practiced for the Congressional Baseball Game for Charity, injuring four people before Capitol Police shot and killed him. Hodgkinson had previously posted a series of quotes critical of President Trump along with the caption, "Trump is a selfish inhuman with delusions of grandeur."*[10]

Theodoridis and Martherus go on to explain that dehumanization can also justify illegal behavior to try to keep the "evil animals" out of power:

> *Even vile conspiracy theories — say, the idea Democrats are trafficking in children inside Comet Ping-Pong pizza — may be easier to believe when attached to individuals we think lack some measure of humanity. If we are willing to describe the other side with dehumanizing metaphors, we may be inclined to accept otherwise unacceptable measures to keep them from gaining political power.[10]*

I'm sure I need not explain that such behavior has only gotten worse over time, and is likely to ramp up even further as the U.S. Presidential election in November 2020 draws near. Indeed, shortly after the Minneapolis police killed George Floyd and violent protests broke out, Trump Tweeted "When the looting starts, the shooting starts," and "The only good Democrat is a dead Democrat." [12]

Where do we go from here?

Research on dehumanization makes it very clear, as the original article points out, that such speech increases the likelihood that the conflict will spin out of control and escalate into violence by weakening the taboos that protect us all from hate crimes and crimes against humanity. Once people begin thinking of their opponents as sub-human, it is much easier to start treating them in ways they would never treat a fellow human, paving the way for mass atrocities. It's hard to think that something like that could happen in the United States. But the seeds are being planted, and the shoots of deep hatred are starting to show. This is likely a major reason why the killing of George Floyd (and associated acts of police brutality) have sparked such outrage. It revealed that police officers, who are responsible for protecting us from hate crimes, are in fact, guilty of those crimes. It is imperative, NOW, that we strongly disavow dehumanizing speech and actions--coming from all sides (not just "the other" side) and work to mend relationships between our increasingly adversarial groups.

-- Heidi Burgess, June, 2020.

Notes

[1] Susan Opotow, "Aggression and Violence," in *The Handbook of Conflict Resolution: Theory and Practice*, eds. M. Deutsch and P.T. Coleman. (San Francisco: Jossey-Bass, 2000), 417.

[2] Susan Opotow, "Drawing the Line: Social Categorization, Moral Exclusion, and the Scope of Justice." In *Cooperation, Conflict, and Justice: Essays Inspired by the Work of Morton Deutsch*, eds. B.B. Bunker and J.Z. Rubin. (New York: Sage Publications, 1995), 347.

[3] Morton Deutsch, "Justice and Conflict," in *The Handbook of Conflict Resolution: Theory and Practice*, eds. M. Deutsch and P.T. Coleman. (San Francisco: Jossey-Bass, 2000), 51.

[4] Janice Gross Stein, "Image, Identity and Conflict Resolution," in *Managing Global Chaos: Sources of and Responses to International Conflict*, eds. Chester A. Crocker, Fen Osler Hampson, and Pamela R. Aall. (Herndon, VA: USIP Press, 1996), 94.

[5] Jeffrey Z. Rubin and Dean G. Pruitt. *Social Conflict: Escalation, Stalemate, and Settlement,* 2nd Edition. (New York: McGraw Hill College Division, 1994), 99.

[6] Ibid., 103.

[7] Ibid., 100.

[8] Ibid., 104.

[9] Opotow, "Drawing the Line," 349.

[10] Alexander Theodoridis and James Martherus. "Trump is not the only one who calls opponents 'animals.' Democrats and Republicans do it to each other." *The Washington Post.* May 21, 2018. https://www.washingtonpost.com/news/monkey-cage/wp/2018/05/21/trump-isnt-the-only-one-who-calls-opponents-animals-democrats-and-republicans-do-it-to-each-other/. Accessed June 29, 2020.

[11] Ben Armstrong. "The Dehumanization of Republicans." Ben Armstrong's Blog. https://wsau.com/blogs/ben-armstrong-blog/20344/the-dehumanization-of-republicans/. Accessed June 29, 2020.

[12] Aaron Blake. "'The only good Democrat is a dead Democrat.' 'When the looting starts, the shooting starts.' Twice in 25 hours, Trump tweets conspicuous allusions to violence.". *The Washington Post*. May 29, 2020. https://www.washingtonpost.com/politics/2020/05/28/trump-retweets-video-saying-only-good-democrat-is-dead-democrat/ Accessed June 29, 2020.

Viewpoint 4

> *"There is no part of the world that can consider itself immune from the risk of genocide."*

No Country Is Immune to the Risk of Genocide

United Nations

The following viewpoint from the United Nations (UN) explains assertions from then-Secretary-General Special Adviser to the United Nations Adama Dieng stating that genocide is a risk for every country, not just certain regions. The former Secretary-General contends that mass atrocities have taken place in recent times as they have in the past and argues that not enough countries in the international community are working to prevent this violence. He asserts that it is the collective responsibility of all UN Member States and the international community as a whole to prevent genocide. The United Nations is an intergovernmental agency that aims to promote international peace and security.

As you read, consider the following questions:

1. According to former Secretary-General Adama Dieng, which genocides offer lessons to prevent further genocidal violence?

2. How did the Rwandan genocide start, as stated in this viewpoint?
3. Based on this viewpoint, do you think Adama Dieng believes enough is being done to stop genocides?

Not a single country is immune to the risk of genocide, said the United Nations Secretary-General's Special Adviser on Prevention of Genocide today as he marked the 66th anniversary of the signing of the 1948 Genocide Convention.

"As we continue to fight and to realize the objectives, we pay tribute to the millions of men and women who have lost their lives to genocide," said Mr. Adama Dieng as he briefed reporters at UN Headquarters in New York, as part of a series of events in the run-up to Human Rights Day, commemorated annually on 10 December.

"We owe to them and to ourselves and future generations to realize a world free of genocide. We are still far from that, but we aim to make it happen," he added.

Genocide must and can be prevented if we have the will of applying the lessons learned from Rwanda, Srebrenica, and the Holocaust. It is important to identify risk factors that would lead to genocide rather than to wait to when people are being killed.

The Holocaust did not start with the gas chambers and the Rwandan genocide did not start with the slayings. It started with the dehumanization of a specific group of persons.

Genocide is defined by the UN as a crime that is committed against members of a national, ethnic or religious group solely because they are members of that group. Genocide also entails there being intent to exterminate a particular group.

Genocide is when "you are being killed not for what you have done, but for who you are," Mr. Dieng explained.

Currently, 140 Member States are party to the UN Convention on the Prevention and Punishment of Genocide, which was adopted in 1948.

On Thursday, Mr. Dieng's office along with the Permanent Missions of Italy and Tanzania will launch a new Framework of Analysis for Atrocity Crimes which will focus on early warning signs and prevention strategies.

"We know from our experience that genocide is not a single event but a process that takes time, planning and resources which could be halted at any stage," he said.

Marking the anniversary of Convention is an opportunity to renew our commitment to prevent genocide. "We must accept that there is no part of the world that can consider itself immune from the risk of genocide and all regions and all States must build resilience to these crimes," the Special Adviser noted.

It is the collective responsibility of Member States, international institutions, civil society as well as the media to prevent such crimes.

He said that in 2005 world leaders committed to protecting populations who are at risk of genocide through the R2P, or 'responsibility to protect' initiative, now an international norm that addresses the failure to prevent and stop genocides, war crimes, ethnic cleansing and crimes against humanity.

But the question remains why some States have been ready to address genocide and in some cases even prevent it, while others have, unfortunately, failed to do so.

"We are still unable to protect people in Syria from human rights violations," he said, adding that had the Security Council acted when the uprising against the Syrian Government was still peaceful, the current and devastating situation might look different.

"Would we still have seen the rise of the barbaric group like ISIL[Islamic State in Iraq and the Levant]? Such groups do not come from nowhere," Mr. Dieng said.

As for other conflicts, he said atrocious crimes in South Sudan and the Central African Republic (CAR) are being committed based on the issue of identity because they are easily manipulated to generate fear, hatred, and violence.

"We need to think about the significance of the Genocide Convention and do more on the promise of 'never again.' We need political leadership from Member States and the courage to take steps that are not always easy," he said.

When asked about the recent decision by the International Criminal Court (ICC) to drop the charges of crimes against humanity for Kenyan President Uhuru Kenyatta, Mr. Dieng said that he respected the independence of the Court. Accountability for gross human rights violations which occurred in Kenya is important. Victims are waiting for justice.

Answering a question on Gaza, he said he was not here to make a legal determination of genocide but analyse the risk of genocide. Last summer's conflict may have led to crimes against humanity or war crimes. He was aware of Israel's disproportionate military response. But when you send rockets from a civilian area, like Hamas did, that is a crime as well.

When asked about crimes committed during the time of United States intervention in Iraq, he said that the American soldiers were indicted and flown over to the United States to face justice. This is an example of a country that has no capacity to bring to justice criminals.

On Ukraine, he said that the claims by civilians of genocide in the eastern part of the country, he reiterated that no region in the world is immune to atrocious crimes and called for all efforts to protect the rights of minorities in Ukraine.

He also responded to questions on the treatment of the Tamils in Sri Lanka, increasing anti-Semitism in Europe, and Islamophobia.

Viewpoint 5

> *"While genocide is unlikely in the United States, atrocities which amount to mass violations of human rights and crimes against humanity are evident."*

Warning Signs of Mass Violence Exist in the United States

Nadia Rubaii and Max Pensky

In this viewpoint, Nadia Rubaii and Max Pensky examine examples of rhetoric and political policies that took place under the Trump administration that point to dehumanization and the threat of crimes against humanity. Through considering the 10 stages of genocide proposed by Gregory H. Stanton, founder of the nonprofit Genocide Watch, the authors argue that recent behaviors suggest that the United States is in the middle stages—discrimination, dehumanization, organization, and polarization—and this puts the U.S. at risk of mass violence. In fact, the authors argue that the Trump administration's detainment of immigrants and separation of children from families is a prime example of this. Nadia Rubaii is an associate professor of public administration at Binghamton University, where Max Pensky is a professor of philosophy. They co-direct the Institute for Genocide and Mass Atrocity Prevention.

"Preventing Crimes Against Humanity in the U.S.," by Nadia Rubaii and Max Pensky, The Conversation, June 22, 2018. https://theconversation.com/preventing-crimes-against-humanity-in-the-us-98679.

As you read, consider the following questions:

1. What past examples of genocidal violence in the U.S. do the authors cite?
2. According to George H. Stanton, do the processes that are considered the stages of genocide necessarily mean that mass violence will occur?
3. How is polarization defined in this viewpoint?

There are those who say that comparing President Donald Trump's rhetoric to that of Adolf Hitler is alarmist, unfair and counterproductive.

And yet, there has been no dearth of such comparisons nearly one and a half years into his term.

Many commentators have also drawn parallels between the conduct and language of Trump supporters and Holocaust-era Nazis. Recent news of ICE agents separating immigrant families and housing children in cages have generated further comparisons by world leaders, as well as Holocaust survivors and scholars. Trump's use of the word "infest" to refer to immigrants coming to the U.S. is particularly striking. Nazis referred to infestations of Jewish vermin, and Rwandan Hutu's labeled Tutsi as cockroaches.

In August 2017, in the wake of the Charlottesville violence, the president used a familiar rhetorical strategy for signaling support to violent groups. He referenced violence on "both sides," implying moral equivalence between protesters calling for the removal of Confederate statues and those asserting white supremacy. His comments gave white supremacists and neo-Nazis the implied approval of the president of the United States.

Many of these groups explicitly seek to eliminate from the U.S. African-Americans, Jews, immigrants and other groups, and are willing to do so through violence. As co-directors of Binghamton University's Institute for Genocide and Mass Atrocity Prevention, we emphasize the importance of recognizing and responding to early warning signs of potential genocide and other atrocity crimes.

Usually, government officials, scholars and nongovernmental organizations look for these signals in other parts of the world—Syria, Sudan or Burma.

But what about the U.S.? President Trump's executive order halting family separations provides Congress an opportunity to act. How the legislators respond will be an important indicator of where the U.S. is headed.

Is It Possible in the U.S.?

The term "genocide" invokes images of gas chambers the Nazis used to exterminate Jews during World War II, the Khmer Rouge killing fields of Cambodia and thousands of Tutsi bodies in the Kagera River in Rwanda. On that scale and in that manner, genocide is highly unlikely in the United States.

But genocidal violence can happen in the U.S. It has happened. Organized policies passed by elected U.S. lawmakers have targeted both Native Americans and African-Americans. Public policies defined these groups as not fully human and not protected by basic laws. Current policies treat immigrants the same way.

The threat of genocide is present wherever a country's political leadership tolerates or even encourages acts with an intent to destroy a racial, ethnic, national or religious group, whether in whole or in part. While genocide is unlikely in the United States, atrocities which amount to mass violations of human rights and crimes against humanity are evident. The U.N. defines crimes against humanity as any "deliberate act, typically as part of a systematic campaign, that causes human suffering or death on a large scale." Unlike genocide, it does not need to include the actual destruction or intent to destroy a group.

According to Holocaust survivors, the current visual and audio accounts of children separated from their parents in border detention facilities reminds them of practices of the Nazis in ghettos and concentration and extermination camps.

The Holocaust took the international community by surprise. In hindsight, there were many signs. In fact, scholars have learned a great deal about the danger signals for the risk of large-scale violence against vulnerable groups.

In 1996, the founder and first president of the U.S.-based advocacy group Genocide Watch, Gregory H. Stanton, introduced a model that identified eight stages—later increased to 10—that societies frequently pass through on the way to genocidal violence and other mass atrocities. Stanton's model has its critics. Like any such model, it can't be applied in all cases and can't predict the future. But it has been influential in our understanding of the sources of mass violence in Rwanda, Burma, Syria and other nations.

The 10 Stages of Genocide

The early stages of Stanton's model include "classification" and "symbolization." These are processes in which groups of people are saddled with labels or imagined characteristics that encourage active discrimination. These stages emphasize "us-versus-them" thinking, and define a group as "the other."

The 10 Stages of Genocide

STAGE	NAME	DESCRIPTION
1	Classification	The differences between people are not respected. There's a division of 'us' and 'them.' This can be carried out through the use of stereotypes, or excluding people who are perceived to be different.
2	Symbolization	This is a visual manifestation of hatred. Jews in Nazi occupied Europe were forced to wear yellow stars to show that they were 'different.'
3	Discrimination	The dominant group denies civil rights or even citizenship to identified groups. The Nuremberg Laws of 1935 in Nazi Germany stripped Jews of their German citizenship and prohibited their employment by the government and by universities.

4	Dehumanization	Those who are perceived as 'different' are treated with no form of human right or personal dignity. During the Genocide in Rwanda, Tutsis were referred to as 'cockroaches'; the Nazis referred to Jews as 'vermin.'
5	Organization	Genocides are always planned. Regimes of hatred often train those who are to carry out the destruction of a people.
6	Polarization	Propaganda begins to be spread by hate groups. The Nazis used the newspaper *Der Stürmer* to spread and incite messages of hate about Jewish people.
7	Preparation	Perpetrators plan the genocide. They often use euphemisms to cloak their intentions, create fear of the victim group and build armies, buy weapons and train their troops and militias.
8	Persecution	Victims are identified and separated out because of their ethnic or religious identity and death lists are drawn up. People are sometimes segregated into ghettos, deported or starved and property is often expropriated. Genocidal massacres begin.
9	Extermination	The hate group murders their identified victims in a deliberate and systematic campaign of violence. Millions of lives have been destroyed or changed beyond recognition through genocide.
10	Denial	The perpetrators or later generations deny the existence of any crime.

Source: Based on Gregory H. Stanton's 10 stages of genocide

As Stanton makes clear, these processes are universally human. They do not necessarily result in a progression toward mass violence. But they prepare the ground for the next stages: active "discrimination," "dehumanization," "organization" and "polarization." These middle stages may be warning signs of an increasing risk of large-scale violence.

Where Are We Now?

Trump's political rhetoric helped propel him into office by playing on the fears and resentments of the electorate. He has used derogatory labels for certain religious and ethnic groups, hinted at dark conspiracies, winked at violence and appealed to nativist and nationalist sentiments. He has promoted discriminatory policies including travel restrictions and gender-based exclusions.

Classification, symbolization, discrimination and dehumanization of Muslims, Mexicans, African-Americans, immigrants, the media and even the political opposition may be leading to polarization, stage six of Stanton's model.

Stanton writes that polarization further drives wedges between social groups through extremism. Hate groups find an opening to send messages that further dehumanize and demonize targeted groups. Political moderates are edged out of the political arena, and extremist groups attempt to move from the former political fringes into mainstream politics.

Do Trump's implied claims of a moral equivalence between neo-Nazis and counterprotesters in Charlottesville move us closer to the stage of polarization?

Does housing children in cages at border detention facilities in the name of deterrence represent a deepening dehumanization?

Certainly, there are reasons for deep concern. Moral equivalence—the claim that when both "sides" in a conflict use similar tactics, then one "side" must be as morally good or bad as the other—is what logicians call an informal fallacy. Philosophers take their red pens to student essays that commit it. But when a president is called on to address his nation in times of political turmoil, the claim of moral equivalence is a lot more than an undergraduate mistake.

Similarly, when warehousing children in cages and tent cities is justified as a policy of deterrence, this is more than an academic policy debate. We suggest this is a deliberate effort to dehumanize and polarize, and an invitation to what may come next.

While the U.S. may not be on the path to genocide in the sense of mass killings, it clearly is engaging in other crimes against humanity—deliberately and systematically causing human suffering on a large scale and violating fundamental human rights.

Responding and Preventing

Polarization is a warning of the increased risk of violence, not a guarantee. Stanton's model also argues that every stage offers opportunities for prevention. Extremist groups can have their financial assets frozen. Hate crimes and hate atrocities can be more consistently investigated and prosecuted. Moderate politicians, human rights activists, representatives of threatened groups and members of the independent media can be provided increased security.

Encouraging responses have come from the international community, the electorate, business leaders and government officials. German Chancellor Angela Merkel condemned the racist and far-right violence displayed in Charlottesville, and U.K. Prime Minister Theresa May harshly criticized Trump's use of moral equivalence. More recently, Pope Francis and the governments of various countries have spoken out about U.S. family separation practices.

The recent withdrawal of the U.S. from the U.N. Human Rights Council suggests that international pressure may not be effective. Domestic actors may have more luck.

Individuals and groups are following the recommendations presented in the Southern Poverty Law Center's guide to combating hate in supporting victims, speaking up, pressuring leaders and staying engaged. Business leaders have also expressed their discontent with Trump's polarizing statements and actions. The American Academy of Pediatrics has gone so far as to label the immigrant family separations a form of mass child abuse.

Local governments are struggling to maintain their status as sanctuary cities or cities of resistance. These cities try to provide refuge for immigrants despite ICE raids and arrests. The general public and politicians of both parties and at all levels are speaking out about the separations, and it appears they may be heard.

In our assessment, these actions represent essential forms of resistance to the movement toward escalating atrocities. The executive order issued by President Trump this week provides the elected representatives in Congress with an important opportunity. Will they be complicit in or act to prevent further atrocities?

It also provides the general public an opportunity to strongly assert a commitment to human rights. How Congress responds will be a clear indicator of whether our democratic checks and balances are functioning to stop atrocities from escalating, or whether we are continuing down a dangerous path.

Viewpoint 6

> *"Nobody is violent just for the sake of being violent. Violence in this context is always a means to an end."*

Genocide Is a Response to Extreme Political Threat

Andrea Bartoli and Mahbubur Rahman

In this viewpoint from the Daily Star, *Dr. Andrea Bartoli and Mahbubur Rahman discuss the Bangladesh Genocide of 1971, in which the government of Pakistan attempted to quell the fight for an independent Bangladesh by committing genocide against Bengali civilians. This was a massive genocide—the biggest since the Holocaust, with 3 million people killed—but because maintaining control of Bangladesh was politically important, the Pakistani government justified these atrocities. Dr. Bartoli says that the same pattern of justifying violence to support state or religious interests exists today. Andrea Bartoli is an international conflict resolution expert and academic at Seton Hall University, and Mahbubur Rahman is a reporter for the* Daily Star.

As you read, consider the following questions:

1. According to this viewpoint, why did the Pakistani military attack Bengali civilians?

"Genocide is very often a response to an extreme political threat," thedailystar.net, March 26, 2015. Reprinted by permission.

2. How do perpetrators of genocide view their victims, according to this viewpoint?
3. What does Andrea Bartoli say about justice in the context of genocides such as the Bangladesh Genocide?

Dr. Andrea Bartoli, Dean of the School of Diplomacy and International Relations of Seton Hall University, talks to Mahbubur Rahman of *The Daily Star* on genocide and its consequences.

The Daily Star (TDS): Please tell us something about the origins of genocide.

Dr. Andrea Bartoli (AB): Genocide is a very old phenomenon. Addressing differences through violence is not a norm but certainly happens often enough. Genocidal violence can be traced back to the very old past. We have historical cases of cities and populations that were wiped out; there are even pre-historical cases of villages that were raided and destroyed. We know that humans have this capacity for destruction. What is specific about genocide, though, is that it is intentional and against a certain group—a national, cultural and/or religious group.

TDS: What is the significance of Bangladesh in this respect?

AB: The case of Bangladesh is a very important one. It happened after the approval in 1948 of the International Convention on the Prevention and Punishment of Crime of Genocide. The importance of this convention is that it gave a name to this phenomenon. So you have something that happened many times but there was no name for it. It was not just the violence of war or an oppressive regime. This was a specific type of violence—intentional attacks against human groups. It is particularly important because when it happened in 1971, the world had a concept of what was happening.

It was a period in which the convention existed formally but there was no real desire on the part of anybody to really act on those words. I describe this as a period of wilful neglect. People knew that the convention existed but they were ignoring the fact. They pretended that the convention never existed. This was particularly true of the Pakistani military that attacked the Bengali population. It was not the first time that an entire population was under oppression by a powerful force. What was different in this case, however, was the military attack against civilian populations. It was unleashed with extreme precision and great effectiveness. The operation was not carried out as part of the civil war; it was actually a response to the electoral results that changed the course of Pakistan forever.

The Pakistani military decided to wage war against Bengali civilians and authorities, and found a popular response against their decision. They lost the war and the capacity to pretend that nothing had happened. The millions of refugees, the thousands of women that were raped, and the hundreds of thousands of families that were affected by the violence recognised the brutality of those nine months.

In many ways, we are still grappling with those memories.

TDS: What do you have to say about the legacy of the genocide in 1971?

AB: There is a connection between the legacy of 1971 and what we are experiencing now. The fundamental question of genocide in 1971 is still alive today because there were people who believed that violence and war could be advantageous for them. Many of these people even believed that it was their duty to commit genocide, be violent and engage in war.

They justified the war on the grounds of state interest and religion. They claimed that the Bengalis were not Muslim enough, and needed to be converted into true Muslims.

Nobody is violent just for the sake of being violent. Violence in this context is always a means to an end. The problem we are facing today is that people still believe that they can use violence, genocide, and war to obtain political results.

TDS: Why do you think people resort to extremist ideologies?

AB: People become convinced that violence is the best solution for them, or in some cases it is their only solution. When they don't make much progress, they start to believe that the use of violence is not only justified but also a duty. To those who commit genocide, the sense of threat and duty is very important. They construct the victims as danger. They view the victim along these lines: 'You are a danger to me. I need to kill you, eliminate you because otherwise I will not exist as I am now or as I would like to exist.' Genocide is very often a response to an extreme political threat.

TDS: How can justice be implemented in this regard?

AB: Humans are a very poor example of the values of justice. True justice comes in a religious sense and spiritual sense. The states that are now calling for prevention of genocide are the same ones that were doing nothing when Bangladeshis were being murdered.

Taking Avijit's case … Even if the perpetrators of Avijit's killing are not caught or brought to justice, greater justice would be when the majority of the population of Bangladesh says, 'Killing is wrong. Killing somebody for saying something is wrong. Killing in the name of Islam is wrong.'

Justice is not only in the hands of specialists, lawyers, judges and prosecutors. Justice is first and foremost a relation between people. Every time we allow the victim to speak, give the victim a voice, and point out when something is wrong or immoral, it makes justice stronger.

Periodical and Internet Sources Bibliography

The following articles have been selected to supplement the diverse views presented in this chapter.

Hannah Beech, "Khmer Rouge's Slaughter in Cambodia is Ruled a Genocide," *New York Times,* November 15, 2018. https://www.nytimes.com/2018/11/15/world/asia/khmer-rouge-cambodia-genocide.html.

Gareth Evans, "Lessons from the Cambodian Genocide," Global Centre for the Responsibility to Protect, July 28, 2020. https://www.globalr2p.org/publications/lessons-from-the-cambodia-genocide/.

Quint Forgey, "Is Putin Committing Genocide in Ukraine?" *Politico*, April 4, 2022. https://www.politico.com/newsletters/national-security-daily/2022/04/04/is-putin-committing-genocide-in-ukraine-00022787.

Katherine Gruspier, "Forensic Legacy of the Khmer Rouge: The Cambodian Genocide," National Institutes of Health (NIH), September 1, 2017. https://www.ncbi.nlm.nih.gov/pmc/articles/PMC6474568/.

Antonio Guterres, "Cambodia: In Visit to Genocide Museum, UN Chief Warns of the Dangers of Hate and Persecution," UN News, November 13, 2022. https://news.un.org/en/story/2022/11/1130537.

Sherry Hamby, "What is Dehumanization, Anyway?" *Psychology Today*, June 21, 2018. https://www.psychologytoday.com/us/blog/the-web-violence/201806/what-is-dehumanization-anyway.

Joshua Hammer, "Bosnia on the Brink," *New York Times,* June 14, 2022. https://www.nytimes.com/2022/06/14/magazine/bosnia-genocide-pyramids.html.

Chico Harlan, "Bosnia is Still Finding Bodies from a Genocide Some Leaders Claim Never Happened," *Washington Post*, February 21, 2022. https://www.brookings.edu/articles/decision-to-intervene-how-the-war-in-bosnia-ended/.

Eweline U. Ochab, "Is Putin Committing Genocide in Ukraine?" *Forbes*, April 4, 2022. https://www.forbes.com/sites/

ewelinaochab/2022/04/04/is-putin-committing-genocide-in-ukraine/?sh=27d6667c557b.

Brian Resnick, "The Dark Psychology of Dehumanization, Explained," *Vox*, March 7, 2017. https://www.vox.com/science-and-health/2017/3/7/14456154/dehumanization-psychology-explained.

George Wright, "Ukraine War: Is Russia Committing Genocide?" BBC News, April 13, 2022. https://www.bbc.com/news/world-europe-61017352.

OPPOSING VIEWPOINTS® SERIES

Chapter 4

Can Genocide Be Prevented?

Chapter Preface

Ever since the term "genocide" was first coined in the mid-20th century, finding ways to prevent future genocides from happening has been a major concern. But in many cases, the media, the public, and even governments turn a blind eye to signs that genocide or other acts of mass violence are occurring. What happens when information about this type of violence actually is presented on TV or shared on social media? People react in different ways, as witnessed by the reaction to the escalating violent events that began in February of 2022 with the start of the Ukraine-Russia war. Being aware of current global situations and learning about the history of genocide are steps that individuals, including students, can take to make a difference.

Genocide is a complex issue, so not surprisingly, the attempts at prevention or prosecution of those responsible for such crimes is challenging. Despite the UN's 1948 Convention on the Prevention and Punishment of the Crime of Genocide's intent to never let genocide occur again after the Holocaust, genocides and acts of mass violence have continued to occur. The International Criminal Court (ICC) in the Hague, Netherlands, was established in 1998 to prosecute individuals in the international community for war crimes, including genocide and other crimes against humanity. However, there have been concerns about the fact that a disproportionate number of the leaders tried for these crimes are from Africa, and very few from Europe, suggesting that Western nations are reluctant to cast a critical eye on the misdeeds of their neighbors. Additionally, the court depends on state cooperation, meaning it is very easy for leaders to avoid being charged by the ICC if they take over or continue to control the government.

For a wide range of reasons, new genocides have continued to happen, and holding leaders accountable for their crimes continues to prove difficult. However, as the viewpoints in this chapter suggest, there is cause for hope as well as concern. Social media helps spread awareness of mass violence and crimes against humanity as they are happening in real time. Additionally, research into genocide has helped determine some of the risk factors for this crime, and as a result the importance of promoting stable governments around the world has been recognized.

The viewpoints in this chapter debate whether genocide can be prevented. Viewpoint authors analyze the problem and outline steps that various governments have taken to curtail violence and chaos. They also suggest ways that individuals, communities, and governments can work together to prevent tragedy in the future.

Viewpoint 1

> *"Common humanity is the foundation of human rights."*

Countries Must Embrace the Universal Declaration of Human Rights

Laksiri Fernando

In the following viewpoint, Dr. Laksiri Fernando analyzes the Universal Declaration of Human Rights—a landmark international human rights document adopted by the UN General Assembly in 1948—point by point and explains concepts that are important to the international community. He contends that all individuals deserve certain rights simply on the basis of being human. He also maintains that this may be taken for granted in Western developed nations, but developing nations have had and continue to have great difficulty providing these conditions. Consequently, the struggle for basic human rights around the world continues to this day. Dr. Laksiri Fernando is a retired senior professor at the University of Colombo in Sri Lanka.

As you read, consider the following questions:

1. What are the five principles of human rights, as stated in this viewpoint?
2. In the application of human rights, what distinctions does the author argue should be avoided?

"Universal Declaration of Human Rights & Its Relevance to Our Lives," by Dr. Laksiri Fernando, Colombo Telegraph, December 13, 2021. Reprinted by permission.

3. What should people expect to have as a standard of living, as explained by the author?

The universal Declaration of Human Rights (UDHR) is now 73 years old. It was adopted by the United Nations on December 10, 1948. At that time, there were only 58 member states. Now there are 193 member states as a consequence of the decolonization in Asia and Africa, the breakup of previously large states like the Soviet Union, and various other reasons.

The UN Charter is the foundation of the present international order between member states. Adopted in 1945, the Universal Declaration can be considered its principal manifesto looking after the matters of people's human rights. The immediate reason for human rights taking a principal focus of the UN was the tragic experiences of fascism and harrowing atrocities during World War II. However, when the Declaration was drafted, the perspective was futuristic.

As a declaration, the UDHR does not have a strict legal binding on member states but appears a most accepted and appreciated manifesto internationally. Academically speaking, there can be some weaknesses or imbalances in the UDHR. However, there is nothing to reject or object of its principles or articles.

Consisting of 30 simply written Articles, it covers the meaning of human rights, their roots, relevance to all peoples internationally, and most importantly, five principal aspects of human rights as civil, political, economic, social, and cultural rights. The Declaration is available in over 500 languages including in Sinhala and Tamil. The Sri Lanka Foundation and Foundation Institute (SLF/SLFI) were instrumental in translating the Declaration into Tamil and Sinhala.

Since 1948, while the UN has adopted nearly 200 further declarations, covenants, and conventions, the International Covenant on Civil and Political Rights (ICCPR) and the International Covenant on Economic, Social and Cultural Rights (ICESCR) can be considered the main international instruments transforming the UDHR into more practical relevance.

Some of the important guidelines in promoting human rights are the following, as referred in the Preamble.

- "Inherent dignity and equal and inalienable rights of all members of the human family are the foundation of freedom, justice and peace in the world."
- "Disregard and contempt for human rights have resulted in barbarous acts which have outraged the conscience of mankind."
- "If man is not to be compelled to have recourse, as a last resort, to rebellion against tyranny and oppression, human rights should be protected by the rule of law."

While reflecting on the above, Sri Lanka and Sri Lankans can ask the question themselves: Have they done the necessary to promote human rights during the last 73 years? Yes, there was a time when governments and various other public agencies promoted human rights education and training. Human rights were even part of school curricula at one time. The Sri Lankan army also had an extensive human rights programme from 2000 –2005. But unfortunately, all these have taken a backstage now. The purpose of celebrating the World Human Rights Day this year should be to rejuvenate these efforts again and determine to promote and protect human rights in the country.

Important Principles

In understanding human rights, and their relevance to our lives, articles in the Declaration are particularly important. Common humanity is the foundation of human rights. Article 1 enunciates this concept perhaps a little idealistically saying, "All human beings are born free and equal in dignity and rights. They are endowed with reason, and conscience and should act towards one another in a spirit of brotherhood."

Birth undoubtedly has some fundamental equality. But unfortunately, we are born into unequal societies and some people are born also with disabilities. A realistic view of human rights should accept that. Otherwise, we will be in a dream world. Yes, we all have or should have "reason and conscience" and that is something we all should try to promote ourselves and among our children, siblings, and friends. That is the meaning of the second sentence.

In the application of human rights there should not be any distinction as to "race, colour, sex, language, religion, political or other opinion, national or social origin, property, birth or other status," (Article 2). In the second sentence of the article, it also adds rejection of discrimination based on the country of origin. In the case of immigration, this principle should apply, although it is disregarded by many countries. What are the other key principles?

- "Everyone has the right to life, liberty, and security of person."
- "No one shall be subjected to torture or to cruel, inhuman or degrading treatment or punishment."
- "All are equal before the law and are entitled without any discrimination to equal protection of the law."

The above and many others in articles 6 to 17 have articulated what we normally call civil rights. Do we have them in our countries? This is something we should ponder in "celebrating" the Human Rights Day.

Political Rights

Political rights may be more important today in all countries because of trends towards authoritarianism. While "everyone has the right to freedom of thought, conscience and religion" in equality and without discrimination, "everyone also has the right to freedom of opinion and expression." This right includes "freedom to hold opinions without interference and to seek, receive and impart information and ideas through any media and regardless of frontiers."

Freedom of the media, journalists, publications, research, and teaching are cornerstones of freedom of opinion. In the politically active sphere, "everyone has the right to freedom of peaceful assembly and association." This includes the right to form trade unions, political parties, oppositions, and civil society organizations.

For a democratic political system, Article 21 can be considered most important. The meaning of "everyone has the right to take part in the government of his/her country, directly and/or through freely chosen representatives" is far reaching although not understood or explained properly. This right is not limited to election time, but all times and the public authorities are duty bound to listen and seek public opinion on all important issues. The principle that "everyone has the right of equal access to public service in his/her country" which appears in the same article has relevance in Sri Lanka today where the public service is ostracized and castigated due to its so-called failure to produce profits!

The concept of "sovereignty of the people" has come to our constitution from the same article which further says, "the will of the people shall be the basis of the authority of government. This will/shall be expressed in periodic and genuine elections which shall be by universal and equal suffrage and shall be held by secret vote or by equivalent free voting procedures."

Economic and Social Rights

Everyone, as a member of society, has the right to social security. That is the basis of economic, social, and cultural rights. "Economic, social, and cultural rights are indispensable for his/her dignity and the free development of his/her personality." That is what the Declaration says in Article 22.

Although in liberal democratic countries many civil and political rights are safeguarded, economic and social rights are lagging behind, except in countries where welfare policies or social democracy prevails. It is naturally difficult in developing countries to fulfil economic and social rights except through international cooperation. However, international cooperation for the "right to development" is largely neglected by Western countries and multilateral organizations today. The UN might be the only hope for the countries with poverty, malnutrition, health issues, vast unemployment, and large income gaps.

Right to employment is the crucial requirement in poor countries. If this is not supplied in the private sector, the State should come forward and supply it through the public sector. This has been the policy in Sri Lanka in the past, but is threatened on various grounds at present.

The Declaration says, "Everyone has the right to work, to free choice of employment, to just and favorable conditions of work and to protection against unemployment." Everyone has the right to equal pay for equal work without any discrimination. This is also not fulfilled in Sri Lanka especially in the case of women and the estate workers. The full range of economic rights have never been achieved in Sri Lanka or in other countries. The following article is the basic criteria.

"Everyone has the right to a standard of living adequate for the health and well-being of himself and of his family, including food, clothing, housing and medical care and necessary social services, and the right to security in the event of unemployment, sickness, disability, widowhood, old age or other lack of livelihood in circumstances beyond his control."

The above quick description of the Universal Declaration shows that human rights are still a pending struggle, particularly in the economic and social sphere. All progressive political parties should embrace human rights in their policies and programs without confining themselves to changing one government against the other. Change of governments are necessary but with a perspective of establishing and reinstating a broad range of human rights in a progressive manner, mobilizing people through awareness, education, and action.

Viewpoint 2

> *"The European Union, United States and other allies must find ways to deter further war crimes and crimes against humanity by Russia in Ukraine."*

Genocide or Not, It Is Essential to Acknowledge War Crimes and Crimes Against Humanity

Dominique Fraser

In the following viewpoint, Dominique Fraser argues that Russia is not committing genocide in the Ukraine. She maintains that Russia is committing war crimes and crimes against humanity and to label these crimes a genocide may actually backfire and not help the global community to act in defense of Ukraine. She argues that it is important to acknowledge that these are war crimes, and that they must be punished as such. Fraser outlines ways that countries and governments can help the victims of war crimes and how to prevent further escalation of such violence. Dominique Fraser works at the Asia Society Policy Institute in Australia as a research associate.

"Russia is committing atrocity crimes in Ukraine, but not genocide," by Dominique Fraser, Lowy Institute, March 16, 2022. Reprinted by permission. This article first appeared in The Interpreter, published by the Lowy Institute, Sydney.

As you read, consider the following questions:

1. According to Fraser, is Russia committing genocide in Ukraine?
2. What is a crime against humanity, as defined by this viewpoint?
3. How can atrocity crimes be escalated, according to the author?

Russia is committing atrocity crimes in Ukraine, but they do not constitute genocide. While that distinction matters little to people caught up in this brutal armed conflict, analysts and policymakers must be aware of the difference and tailor their response accordingly.

The use of cluster munitions, attacks on humanitarian corridors, and the targeting of hospitals are just some of the horrific tactics used by Russia in Ukraine. Some within Ukraine have termed these atrocity crimes to be genocide. President Volodymyr Zelensky called Russia's strike on a children's hospital the "ultimate evidence" for genocide, a word that has also been invoked by journalists and analysts. However, these acts likely constitute war crimes and crimes against humanity rather than genocide.

War crimes are grave breaches of the Geneva Convention and other serious violations of the laws and customs of international armed conflict. A crime against humanity is an act—such as murder, rape, and torture—committed "as part of a widespread or systematic attack directed against any civilian population."

Genocide differs from other horrific crimes because it involves an "intent to destroy" a group of people as such, meaning that people are targeted for annihilation based on their nationality, ethnicity, race or religion. While the atrocity crimes in Ukraine are shocking, there is no evidence at the time of writing that they are targeted. Bombs are falling on civilians and their infrastructure regardless of their identity. Nor is there evidence of a plan to destroy

Ukrainians as a group. Ukrainians within Russia and elsewhere are not targeted.

For people in Ukraine, the distinction between the different types of atrocity crimes makes little difference and the invocation of genocide as a rallying cry for greater international action is understandable. (Although unfortunately there is little evidence that a recognition of genocide leads to more robust international action and there is debate what such action could be in Ukraine.)

For analysts and policymakers, the distinction does matter.

High-ranking Russian decision-makers for atrocity crimes must be named and reminded that violating international law can lead to criminal prosecution.

The UN Genocide Convention Explained

The Convention on the Prevention and Punishment of the Crime of Genocide (Genocide Convention) is an international law instrument that codifies genocide as a crime under International Law. It was adopted by the General Assembly on 9 December 1948. Currently, over 140 states are party to the convention.

Article II of the convention defines the crime of genocide to mean any of the following acts

> "committed with intent to destroy, in whole or in part, a national, ethnical, racial or religious group, as such:
> *Killing members of the group;*
> *Causing serious bodily or mental harm to members of the group;*
> *Deliberately inflicting on the group conditions of life calculated to bring about its physical destruction in whole or in part;*
> *Imposing measures intended to prevent births within the group;*
> *Forcibly transferring children of the group to another group.*"

The Convention states that genocide is a crime that could be committed in time of war as well as in time of peace. Punishable acts are listed in Article III.

First, in the absence of an intent to destroy Ukrainians as a group, charges of genocide can easily be dismissed by detractors, while charges of war crimes and crimes against humanity cannot. The Chief Prosecutor of the International Criminal Court has opened an investigation as "there is a reasonable basis to believe that both alleged war crimes and crimes against humanity have been committed."

Second, when designing policies to prevent and stop atrocity crimes, the aim must be to protect those at greatest risk. In Ukraine, that means focusing on people on the ground regardless of nationality, rather than Ukrainians as a group.

So, what can policymakers do to protect all people in Ukraine from war crimes and crimes against humanity? While there has

History of the Genocide Convention

- In 1947, the Secretary-General, assisted with the Division of Human Rights and three experts of International Criminal Law, presented a first draft convention accompanied with a commentary (E/447).
- In 1948, Economic and Social Council resolution 117 (VI) established the Ad Hoc Committee on Genocide, which created a second draft Convention with commentaries (E/794).
- From September to December 1948, the Sixth Committee considered this second draft at the third session of the General Assembly and recommended to the General Assembly for adoption an amended version of the draft convention (A/760, p.9).
- On 9 December 1948, at its 3rd session (A/PV.179), the General Assembly adopted the Genocide Convention by unanimous vote (A/RES/260(III)). It was opened for signature on 11 December 1948 and entered into force on 12 January 1951.

The Secretary-General of the United Nations is the Depositary of the agreement. Therefore, the text and status of the agreement, including the signatories and parties to the treaty, can be found on the UN Treaty Information website, in the Multilateral Treaties Deposited with the Secretary-General (MTDSG) database, otherwise known as the Status of Treaties database.

"What is the Genocide Convention?" United Nations, July 6, 2022.

been near universal condemnation of Russia's aggression, not all countries have reacted as decisively as the European Union, the United States and some others. China and India in particular have faced criticism for their ongoing tacit support for Russia. Yet, some of their own citizens—including many Indian international students—are still trapped in Ukraine and are at risk of atrocity crimes precisely because they are indiscriminate. These countries should use their existing diplomatic channels to put pressure on Russia to observe international law.

The European Union's quick and comprehensive policies to protect people fleeing Ukraine has been lauded, while some have pointed out the stark contrast to how Europe has received refugees from places such as Syria, Afghanistan, and Iraq. While invoking the Temporary Protection Directive protects Ukrainian nationals, stateless persons, and third-party nationals who have resided in Ukraine on a long-term basis, the European Union must ensure that its officers on the ground are aware of this policy and assist the over 400,000 foreign nationals in Ukraine. Scenes such as those seen at the Polish border, where citizens of other countries were prevented from fleeing indiscriminate violence, must not be repeated.

High-ranking Russian decision-makers for atrocity crimes must be named and reminded that violating international law can lead to criminal prosecution, even in the context of domestic impunity: the ICC, international criminal tribunals, and national courts under the principle of "universal jurisdiction" have indicted heads of state and government, army chiefs-of-staff, government ministers, and many others for atrocity crimes. To be prosecuted for war crimes, there is no requirement to have had a special intent to destroy a group (as with genocide) and no requirement to have known of a systematic or widespread attack (as with crimes against humanity). Following orders is also no defence.

Atrocity crimes are more likely to escalate and become targeted if perpetrators act against a group that has been dehumanised. Russians must be reminded that they share close ties with

Ukrainians, who have long been regarded as brothers and sisters. In this context, analysts and policymakers must watch out for signs of escalating hate speech against Ukrainians as a group.

The European Union, United States and other allies must find ways to deter further war crimes and crimes against humanity by Russia in Ukraine. A debate on whether the atrocity crimes constitute genocide is a distraction from this aim and can have unintended consequences for people caught up in the violence.

Viewpoint 3

"Strong liberal democracies not only avoid war with one another, but also have much lower levels of civil conflict, deadly terrorism, attacks against women, violent crime, and poverty."

Democracies Decrease the Risk of Genocide by Avoiding War and Conflict

Democracy Digest

In the following viewpoint, Democracy Digest asserts that democracies work to lessen the chance of having genocides develop by avoiding war and civil conflicts. This is because these governments realize that genocide can manifest out of war. Democracy Digest explains through many examples how democracies do this by considering arguments from experts on foreign policy. Additionally, the viewpoint argues that emerging democracies should be supported by established democracies and encouraged to participate in international politics, which will help strengthen democracy in these countries and make them part of the international community. Democracy Digest is an online daily blog of the National Endowment for Democracy.

"Why liberal democracies avoid war, reduce civil conflict," Democracy Digest, September 21, 2017. Reprinted by permission.

As you read, consider the following questions:

1. How did the Kellogg-Briand Pact help prevent conflict, as reported in this viewpoint?
2. What is one reason that interstate war has declined, according to the author?
3. As reported by the viewpoint, do gender equal societies experience less conflict?

International Peace Day is an appropriate occasion for assessing democracy's contribution to peace and security.

The Kellogg-Briand Pact of 1928, also known as the Paris Peace Pact, does not have a good reputation, for obvious reasons, notes Council on Foreign Relations analyst Max Boot. But Yale law professors Oona A. Hathaway and Scott J. Shapiro contend in their provocative new book, *The Internationalists: How a Radical Plan to Outlaw War Remade the World*, that the naysayers are wrong," he writes for the *New York Times*:

> They claim that while "it did not end war between states," the Kellogg-Briand Pact did mark "the beginning of the end." More than that, "it reshaped the world map, catalyzed the human rights revolution, enabled the use of economic sanctions as a tool of law enforcement, and ignited the explosion in the number of international organizations that regulate so many aspects of our daily lives." Oh, and it led to "the replacement of one international order with another."

Many reasons have been given for the decline of interstate war over the past 70 years, Boot adds:

> They include aversion to the bloodletting of two world wars; the decline of racism, which once justified wars of colonial conquest; the development of nuclear weapons, which make a great-power conflict less likely; the rise of American dominance, which has been employed to stop aggression like Iraq's 1990 invasion of Kuwait; and the spread of democracy and free trade, which make states more likely to cooperate than to fight.

Strong liberal democracies not only avoid war with one another, but also have much lower levels of civil conflict, deadly terrorism, attacks against women, violent crime, and poverty, according to a new analysis, launched last week at the Brookings Institution by former U.S. Secretary of State Madeleine Albright and former Tunisian Prime Minister Mehdi Jomaa. The report, "Liberal democracy and the path to peace and security," is the final report of the Democracy and Security Dialogue held under the auspices of the Community of Democracies.

"Instead of closing our societies and limiting civil liberties, political leaders are better off addressing the root causes of insecurity by repairing the social contract and living up to core democratic principles," As Albright and Jomaa wrote for DefenseOne. "Similarly, on the international front, our leaders should not embrace authoritarians or turn away from the hard diplomatic work of settling conflicts. Instead, we need to help fragile states advance democratic governance, inclusive politics and human rights."

States at intermediate stages of democratization—hybrid regimes with mixed features of democracy and autocracy, elite-driven patronage systems, and/or weak institutions—are generally the most vulnerable to insecurity, whether from violent crime, terrorism, or entrenched poverty, the report states:

> These are states where there is both weak institutional capacity and weak political legitimacy, which together contribute to a breakdown in the social contract between citizens and the government. This report argues that to foster domestic and international security, and to address the underlying drivers of violent extremism, this social contract must be repaired. It is essential, therefore, to adopt strategies to institutionalize democratic governance, inclusive politics, and human rights in fragile states. Civil society—as independent participants, monitors, and critics of our democratic institutions—are also critical ingredients to any strategy for peace.
>
> Stronger democracies are less prone to civil war for at least two reasons, the report contends;

- First, at the elite level, healthy democratic institutions and regular electoral processes create incentives for political participation by a wide range of ideological actors at relatively low cost, while taking up arms involves much higher costs.
- Second, rebel groups are less likely to find support among citizens if popular grievances are being met through peaceful and credible political processes. Strong autocracies also tend to avoid civil wars because of the repression and co-optation employed by their state institutions.

What Can Be Done

There are good strategies available for preventing and ameliorating civil wars if we are prepared to make the long-term investment in political reforms that address the underlying roots of conflict, the COD report suggests:

- **Widen channels of political participation**: First and foremost, the world's democracies should support broad political participation by a wide range of political actors through credible and transparent mechanisms at all levels of government....
- **Embrace women and youth as partners in security**: Given the strong empirical evidence that more gender-equal societies experience less conflict, the international community should make special efforts to support the participation of women in politics, peace processes, conflict resolution mechanisms, and political negotiations. Special efforts should also be made to incorporate youth in decision-making processes wherever possible....
- **Build strong state capacity**: Creating meritocratic, accessible, and properly resourced state institutions—for example, in the realms of social services or the rule of law—is critical to reducing the risks of conflict associated with states dominated by faction-driven patronage....

- **Prioritize support to emerging democracies**: In deciding how best to assist other states, the international community should prioritize support to countries undertaking genuine political reform or emerging from conflict and committed to the democratic path. States that systematically exclude segments of their populations, and are therefore at higher risk of conflict, deserve special attention. In addition to offering expertise on the design of more inclusive and transparent political systems, the international community should support and protect civil society actors engaged in projects of political, economic, and social liberalization.
- **Prepare the ground for competitive politics**: Post-conflict situations are particularly vulnerable to backsliding and, therefore, should not be rushed into competitive politics without time to prepare the ground for fair electoral processes and peaceful acceptance of electoral results....
- **Carry out civilian-led security sector reforms**: One of the more vexing problems associated with strengthening democracy is achieving state monopoly over the use of force while simultaneously reforming the security sector, especially in countries emerging from civil war. ...

Viewpoint 4

> *"Public trust in government is the essence of good governance."*

Building Trust in Government Decreases Chance of Conflict

Kim Boo-Kyum

In the following viewpoint, Kim Boo-Kyum maintains that for governments to work effectively, the citizens must feel a sense of trust in their government. Other viewpoints have pointed out that well-functioning democracies tend to avoid genocide or other atrocities because they mostly function without political turmoil and conflict. Public engagement in policymaking plays an important role in facilitating this trust and stability. Kim Boo-Kyum outlines in this viewpoint how this works in South Korea. Kim Boo-Kyum is the Minister of the Interior and Safety in the Republic of South Korea.

As you read, consider the following questions:

1. As reported in the viewpoint, who was the first South Korean president to be impeached?
2. Which group of people effectively brought about the impeachment, according to the author?
3. When did South Korea join the Open Government Project?

When citizens trust their government, they are more likely to have faith in the long-term benefits of public policies even if they seem counterproductive in the short term.

When Zigong asked Confucius about the essence of government, the master replied: "Sufficient food, a strong army, and the trust of the people.... without the trust of the people, no government could survive." Public trust in government is the essence of good governance. It defines the relationship between citizens and government and determines the acceptability and effectiveness of public policies.

When citizens trust their government, they are more likely to have faith in the long-term benefits of public policies even if they seem counterproductive in the short term. A government faced with unforeseen challenges will have more leeway in policymaking if the people are confident their government will lead the nation in the right direction. Losing public trust means ineffective policymaking. It may even put governments in peril.

Last year, Korea saw this unfold in real time. President Park Geun-hye had been losing public support due to failed responses to the 2014 Sewol ferry disaster and the 2015 MERS outbreak. An influence-peddling scandal in 2016 involving her longtime confidante was the final blow. With impeachment unanimously upheld by Constitutional Court in March 2017, Park became Korea's first democratically elected leader to fail to complete a five-year term.

The makers of this remarkable history that fascinated the world were none other than the Korean people, who held candlelight rallies every weekend for five months demanding the president step down. Over 16 million people joined protests across the nation. What united these massive gatherings was the people's shared hope for a new nation. The peaceful protests moved even many then-ruling party members in favor of impeachment. The successful transfer of power brought on by candlelight was hailed as a modern-day Glorious Revolution.

The current administration owes much of its success to the "candlelight democracy." Moon Jae-in was elected by a landslide in May 2017 and continues to enjoy high approval ratings. However, it's too early to sit on our laurels. Koreans have learned that a democratically elected leader alone is no guarantee of a true democracy. The Moon administration must learn to listen to the public and deliver on its promise of a meaningful democracy. Only then will the president's current popularity translate into lasting public confidence in the overall government.

The current administration understands this challenge, as reflected in its five-year policy agenda unveiled in July 2017. Although every Korean president since 1987 has been elected by democratic procedures, state affairs were still administered in a government-centered way. The 2016 candlelight protests ushered in "an era of the people," where the people are no longer subjects to be ruled, but owners of their nation playing active roles in politics. Korean democracy must evolve from purely elections into a true democracy in which popular sovereignty is maintained.

The Moon administration started by accepting over 180,000 proposals from citizens through a new communication channel "Gwanghwamun 1st Street" at the policy planning stage and incorporated those ideas into the five-year roadmap. The Moon administration announced "A People's Country, a Just Korea" as a national vision and set "A Government of the People" as the most important of its five policy goals. The key is to shift from closed, unilateral decision making to an open public process in which policies are made based on open discussion and public engagement.

The government formed a public opinions committee on the longstanding controversial issue of new nuclear power plant construction as an experiment of deliberative democracy. Furthermore, plans for government-wide support is under way for a "social innovation," the process of solving social issues with innovative ideas through public participation.

Expanding public participation and deliberative decision-making may seem chaotic and inefficient in the short term.

However, it is a necessary growing pain for reaching a consensus based on rational, fact-based discussion rather than appealing to partisan prejudice and antagonism that have long characterized Korea's political discourse. With enough practice, a trust-based partnership between government and citizens will be achieved in the long term.

Civic participation, government-citizen partnership and deliberative democracy are in line with the values pursued by the Open Government Partnership (OGP). OGP provides an exemplary mechanism to encourage public participation throughout the policymaking process, from agenda setting to evaluation. It holds national governments accountable to the international community for their pledge to deliver an open government.

The Korean government joined the OGP in 2011 and recently launched an OGP Forum. Government ministries and civil society organizations are to co-create the entire process, from establishing the National Action Plan to reviewing its implementation.

The Korean government will continue to make efforts to present more ambitious commitments in the NAP and learn from other countries pioneering in the area of open government. I am confident this is a path to true democracy.

As Robert Axelrod suggests in *The Evolution of Cooperation*, positive interactions repeated over the long term can lead to the formation of trust and greater cooperation. Korea is witnessing numerous positive interactions between the government and citizens. I believe this is the first step on a long journey to creating trust and cooperation.

Viewpoint 3

> *"There are several measures that all nations ought to take to prevent future genocide."*

How to Prevent Genocide in the Future

Alon Ben-Meir

In the following viewpoint, Dr. Alon Ben-Meir argues that even as countries have signed on to the international convention to prevent genocide after World War II, genocides still persist today. Dr. Ben-Meir outlines and examines the motives behind past genocides, retracing the steps in history that led to the violence. He then describes his plan to prevent future genocides, which includes improving education about genocide, publicly acknowledging and speaking out against mass violence and crimes against humanity, and ensuring that the international community monitors violent conflicts. Dr. Alon Ben-Meir is a professor of international relations at New York University and teaches courses on international negotiation and Middle Eastern studies.

As you read, consider the following questions:

1. What are the motives that leaders in the past used to condone genocide, as reported in this viewpoint?
2. How does propaganda play a part in genocide?
3. How can schools play a role in preventing genocide?

"Steps for preventing future genocides," by Alon Ben-Meir, San Diego Jewish World, June 4, 2019. Reprinted by permission.

The phenomenon of genocide has baffled historians for many generations. The question that has been and continues to be asked is what goes through the minds of leaders, however despotic and ruthless, to conclude that committing genocide against their real or perceived enemies will provide them with salvation that only the extermination of other people would bring? And what does that say about us as human beings, who have failed to adopt "never again," sworn to in the wake of World War II, as the mantra to guide us in preventing the occurrences of genocides?

It seems that we settled on the notion that modernity and civilization, and international laws that prohibit crimes against humanity, will be enough to prevent future genocides. To the contrary, modernity is where genocide reached its pinnacle, enabling countries to murder on an assembly line, such as the genocide committed by Germany against the Jews. Obviously, this notion is completely misguided, as is evident by the genocides in Kosovo, the Sudan, and Rwanda that were perpetrated nearly five decades after the conclusion of the second World War.

The various motives that prompted previous leaders to commit such large-scale genocides have not changed, as xenophobia, racism, discrimination, and intolerance remain very much a part of human society. Even a cursory review of what is happening around us at the present, from China to America, suggests that the roots of genocide have not been eradicated. Indeed, as long as we continue to see each other from the prism of a different religion, different color, different race, or different ideology, and blame others for our plight, the prospect of future genocides still looms high.

The genocides that occurred over the past 110 years were motivated by different rationales but led to similar horrifying consequences.

Following the collapse of the Ottoman Empire, the Turks advocated for the formation of an exclusively Turkish Muslim state. The policy of "Turkey for the Turks," and rejection of any nationality that did not subscribe to Islam, led to the decimation of nearly 2.5 million Pontic Greeks and Armenians. In Rwanda, genocide was perceived as the only way to break out of a historical cycle of discrimination and oppression of the Hutu majority by the Tutsi minority.

The Germans believed that they belonged to a superior race—Aryan—while the Jews belonged to an inferior race that threatened to contaminate and pollute German society and culture. Serbia adopted a strong exclusionary ideology, proclaiming that Serbia was for Serbians and that other nationalities should leave or be eliminated. Finally, in Sudan, competition for scarce resources and north Sudan's takeover of the southern Sudanese, the majority of whom are non-Muslim and non-Arab, sparked genocide there.

Methods of Extermination

The states that perpetrated genocide by and large used similar methods to exterminate their enemies. Against the Pontic Greeks, the Ottomans employed massacres, death marches, summary expulsions, arbitrary executions, rape, and forced conscription into labor battalions.

The Serbian military's effort to reassert control over the region was accompanied by atrocities such as the destruction of over 500 villages and killing of an estimated 15,300 civilians. Twenty thousand women were raped, and thousands disappeared. Serbia's response to NATO's intervention was to drive out all the Kosovar Albanians, pushing nearly 1.2 million refugees into neighboring Albania, Macedonia, and Montenegro.

The Turkish policy of exterminating Armenians was carried out under the guise of deportation. Massacres were carried out through mass burnings: 80,000 Armenians in 90 villages were burned in stables and haylofts. Thousands were killed by drowning—women and children would be placed onto boats that were capsized in the Black Sea. Turkish physicians also contributed to the planning and execution of the genocide. All in all, nearly 1.5 million Armenians were extinguished.

In Germany, the Extermination of the Jews, the "Final Solution," began with mobile killing groups called Einsatzgruppen. They gathered Jews town by town, marched them to huge pits, stripped them, lined them up, and shot them with automatic weapons. Immediately following the Wannsee Conference in 1942, Jewish men, women, and children were methodically killed with poisonous gas. More than six million Jews perished over a period of four years.

In Rwanda, an unofficial militia group called the Interahamwe was mobilized; at its peak, this group was 30,000 strong. In addition to brutal mass killings, systematic rape was also used as a weapon of war during the genocide.

The Darfur genocide began in 2003 with the mass murder and rape of people living in Western Sudan, carried out by the Janjaweed, a government-funded group that continued attacks until 2010. The Janjaweed are ethnic Arab militia groups, which would follow government attacks from the air with scorched-earth campaigns, burning villages, and poisoning wells.

Propaganda

Strong pan-Turkish and pan-Islamist propaganda began to appear in the Ottoman press in early August 1914, which alienated and intimidated non-Muslims; the Ottomans believed that the Christian Pontic Greeks were tainting the population and threatening the integrity of the Muslim-majority nation-state. Ottoman authorities created a propaganda campaign, claiming that Armenians were a threat to national security, in part because of some Armenians' support of Russia in the ongoing World War. Because most Turks were illiterate, anti-Armenian propaganda was primarily disseminated in the sermons of Muslim mullahs and by town criers, who labeled Armenians as spies, infidels, and traitors. The promotion of Islamism was critical, as it was the central ideology behind the Armenian and Greek genocides.

One of the major tools of Nazi propaganda was a weekly newspaper, *Der Stürmer* (The Attacker), which proclaimed at the bottom of the front page of each issue, "The Jews are our misfortune!" The newspaper regularly featured cartoons of Jews in which they were caricatured as hooked-nose and ape-like. The Ministry of Public Enlightenment and Propaganda, headed by Joseph Goebbels, employed art, music, theater, films, books, radio, educational materials, and the press. Propaganda encouraged passivity and acceptance of the impending laws against the Jews. Nazi films portrayed Jews as subhuman, wandering parasites, infiltrating Aryan society.

Milosevic's propaganda campaign was based on the Nazis' techniques, with the added power of television. To weld the population together, official propaganda drew on the sources of the Serbian mystique, that of a people who were the mistreated victims and martyrs of history, and that of Greater Serbia, indissolubly linked to the Orthodox religion. Serbian television and radio's repetitive use of pejorative descriptions against Croats, Bosnians, and Albanians quickly became part of common usage.

Hutu extremists in Rwanda also used the media to their benefit. Local officials and government-sponsored radio stations called on ordinary Rwandan civilians to murder their neighbors. Radio was utilized to provide the location of specific Tutsis to be targeted. Radio was also used to justify the genocide; radio hosts discussed discrimination the Hutus suffered under the Tutsis.

In the Nuba Mountains and southern Sudan, crimes against humanity were justified by characterizing victims—Christians by and large—as 'infidels' (kafir). In Darfur, with a mostly Muslim population, a different kind of rationalization for slaughter was required. The regime categorized Darfuris as infidels by connecting them with Judaism, and emphasized that the Fur, Zaghawa, and Massalit were non-Arab; the Zaghawa tribe in particular was portrayed as having Jewish origins. All the tribes were then seen as generally non-Muslim and therefore evil, sub-human, and unable to be trusted.

Measures to Prevent Future Genocide

As we have witnessed, the concept of "never again" that was coined in the wake of the Holocaust and embraced as the mantra for future generations to prevent genocide failed to materialize. Acts of horrifying genocide occurred time and again during the past three decades; Rwanda, Sudan, and Kosovo provide telling examples. What is necessary then is to create awareness, especially among the young generation, about the horrors of genocide that human beings are capable of inflicting on others, and stop pretending that modernity and civilization provide a natural shield against future genocides.

The fact that the current young generation is becoming increasingly less aware of genocides that occurred even two decades ago is extremely worrying. For example, less than 35 percent of Americans are aware there was an Armenian genocide. In Britain, 800 students from 15 schools were asked if they had any knowledge about genocides that occurred since the Holocaust; 81 percent could not name any modern genocide, only 13 percent knew about the Rwandan genocide, 5 percent knew about the atrocities in Bosnia and Cambodia, and a mere 2 percent knew about the Darfur genocide.

There are several measures that all nations ought to take to prevent future genocide, albeit not a single or a combination of such measures can ensure that genocide will never happen again. Nevertheless, we must remain vigilant and do whatever it takes to prevent mass killings.

First, it is crucial that the study of genocide in general be offered as a course that all middle and high school students should be required to take. There is no doubt that learning the history, psychology, motivation, and methodology used to effect mass executions is a necessary step that would help prevent future genocide. In this regard, listening to the stories and experiences of genocide survivors in a classroom setting is critical because unlike reading about genocide (which is vital), sharing the experience of what a survivor has endured, especially when describing the horrifying consequences, humanizes victims and leaves an indelible mark in the minds of the students. In addition, it is necessary to provide books, other printed materials, and videos produced specifically for those age groups to see and feel the level to which human beings are capable of descending.

Second, it is essential that communities hold symposiums and town hall meetings to discuss mass killings with speakers who have personally experienced or are noted authorities on genocide. These should be held on the anniversaries of various genocides, coinciding with public awareness campaigns to ensure that these atrocities are remembered. Organizations focused on educating about and preventing genocide, such as the United States Holocaust Memorial Museum and the Enough Project, should lead the way in holding such events, given their credibility and expertise on the issue of genocide. Inviting the press to cover such events will remind people that we are living in a time when such atrocities can still happen, and that each and every one of us must assume a role, however small, to promulgate knowledge of the unfathomable acts that sadly are still a part of our nature as human beings.

Third, acknowledging that mass murders have in fact occurred, and taking certain measures to prevent it from ever happening again, such as the case with Germany, can go a long way to prevent history from repeating itself by creating a process of reconciliation to heal the wounds. As such, we must not allow countries like Turkey (including its Ottoman predecessors), who committed unspeakable atrocities against the Greeks and Armenians in the wake of World War I, to deny its crimes against humanity with impunity. Even now, Turkey under President Erdogan refuses to acknowledge Turkey's historic crimes. Every country should follow France's and Germany's footsteps and pass laws that make the denial of the Pontic Greek and Armenian genocides a crime punishable by jail time or fine, or both.

Fourth, it is imperative that the UN or EU (preferably the EU to prevent political jockeying), create a commission to monitor conflicts within or between countries that could lead to genocide.

Preventive measures can take place to avert such conflicts from escalating. That is, early intervention could certainly de-escalate tension and mitigate conflicts. For example, early intervention in Rwanda could have prevented the genocide against the Tutsis.

There were clear signs that the tension between the two sides was building up; UN peacekeeping forces commander General Roméo Dallaire notified his superiors in New York that genocide was imminent in a memo now known as the "genocide fax." The fact that nearly 800,000 were slaughtered within a 90-day period was not a spontaneous outburst, but clearly a premeditated scheme that had been in the works for a long period of time.

Finally, in the age of unprecedented social media that allows us to reach millions of people in a few minutes, it should be fully utilized to create greater awareness about genocides. However controversial the use of social media may be, its overwhelming pervasiveness cannot be ignored, and its power must be used to create public awareness about past genocides that would help prevent future gross violations of human rights.

On the same note, companies like Facebook, whose platform was used to incite genocide in Myanmar, and Twitter, which was groundbreakingly used by ISIS to promote its ideology, must be held responsible and be proactive in removing content inciting hatred and violence.

The civil war in Syria that has so far led to the deaths of over 600,000, five million refugees, and as many internally displaced, by definition is not a genocide. However, indiscriminately bombing towns and villages from the air to kill tens of thousands of innocent people is still akin to genocide. When such atrocities can take place both in Syria and in Yemen with little to no effort to stop them, it suggests how inept and indifferent the international community has become, which allows such horrifying carnages to take place.

It is these types of gross human rights violations that are happening with impunity by the perpetrators, along with the ongoing genocides against Rohingya Muslims in Myanmar, and Yazidis, Kurds, and Christians by ISIS, that raise serious questions about our ability to address such horrific crimes. We can, if we only will it. But we are still unwilling to rise and take whatever measures necessary to prevent such atrocities.

What has changed, and what have we learned from previous genocides? Very little. As long as we put our short-sighted political interest above human lives, we prove we have leaned little from history and are condemned to repeat it time and again. We must hold up the mantra of "never again" and act before it's too late.

Viewpoint 6

> *"The work of prevention continues, even after a genocide is over."*

There Are Measures That Can Help Prevent Genocide

Kerry Whigham

In this viewpoint, Kerry Whigham explains that in the nearly 70 years since the Holocaust occurred and the UN Genocide Convention was adopted, genocides have continued to occur because of misunderstandings about what genocide is and how to prevent it. However, in this time, genocide experts have learned some key points in genocide prevention. One thing experts have learned is that genocide takes time to happen, and that it extends beyond mass killings. Recognizing a potential genocide in its early stages—before it has become a genocide—can play a big part in prevention. Kerry Whigham is an assistant professor of genocide and mass atrocity prevention at Binghamton University and Co-Director of its Institute for Genocide and Mass Atrocity Prevention.

As you read, consider the following questions:

1. What are the genocides listed in this viewpoint that were occurring at the time it was originally published?

"Genocides Persist, Nearly 70 Years After the Holocaust—but There Are Recognized Ways to Help Prevent Them," Kerry Whigham, The Conversation, December 2, 2022. https://theconversation.com/genocides-persist-nearly-70-years-after-the-holocaust-but-there-are-recognized-ways-to-help-prevent-them-195260.

2. What are the three stages of genocide prevention mentioned in this viewpoint?
3. What does Whigham suggest the United States should do to help prevent genocide?

The newly formed United Nations passed its first international treaty on Dec. 9, 1948, just three years after the Holocaust ended. The Convention on the Prevention and Punishment of the Crime of Genocide was designed to prevent genocide from ever happening again.

But governments worldwide currently remain far from the goal of preventing genocide—despite 152 of them eventually signing on to the Genocide Convention.

Genocide, meaning actions taken with the intent to destroy a group of people because of their identity, happened again in Cambodia in the 1970s. The communist Khmer Rouge regime tried to kill all ethnic Vietnamese and Cham people in the country, resulting in the deaths of 1.5 million to 3 million people. And it happened in 1994 in Rwanda, when the Hutu ethnic group murdered hundreds of thousands of Tutsis.

Today, governments are also carrying out genocide against ethnic minorities in Myanmar, where the military is killing the Muslim Rohingya people. Many experts and some governments, including the United States, also say genocide is happening in China, where the national government is arbitrarily detaining Uyghur people.

Some human rights experts also say that there is growing evidence Russia is committing genocide against the Ukrainian people.

Genocide has not been prevented, almost 75 years after the Genocide Convention was passed, in part because of a misunderstanding about how genocide happens and what prevention looks like.

As co-director of Binghamton University's Institute for Genocide and Mass Atrocity Prevention and a program director at the Auschwitz Institute for the Prevention of Genocide and Mass Atrocities, I focus on helping students and government officials understand five important things that scholars and practitioners have learned about preventing genocide. Here are those five key points.

Genocide Is a Process, Not an Event

Polish Jewish lawyer Raphael Lemkin first coined the term genocide in 1944. Specifically, the Genocide Convention protects racial, ethnic, religious and national identities.

Although this destruction often happens through mass murder, it can take other forms. It can mean taking children of one group away from their parents and transferring them to another group, for example.

Genocides are not events that happen overnight. They are long-term social and political processes that begin long before mass killing.

For instance, the Nazis did not build death camps immediately when Adolf Hitler was appointed chancellor of Germany in 1933. The Holocaust began with smaller steps, like preventing Jewish people from holding certain jobs, then preventing Jews and non-Jews from marrying each other.

It was not until the late-1930s that the Nazis transitioned to their Final Solution, which called for the destruction of all Jewish people. And the Nazis did not construct the first death camps until 1941. But all these steps over the years constituted what we now call the Holocaust.

Prevention Is Also a Process

When people understand genocide as a process and learn to recognize the early stages that can lead to genocide, there is more opportunity to intervene before people are killed.

Prevention scholars and activists stress a long-term view of prevention that entails three stages.

First, there are actions people can take before genocide occurs to make sure it never happens. This involves identifying which groups of people are at risk of violence, then passing laws, for example, to protect those groups.

A second stage of prevention involves responses to a genocide once it breaks out. This can include using military troops to quash violence. But it could also extend to things like diplomacy, threats of prosecution and economic sanctions.

Finally, a third stage of prevention only occurs when a genocide has already happened. This stage aims to prevent its recurrence. This can include things like truth commissions, which aim to expose and document mass violence or other periods of turmoil, trials against the perpetrators or reparations to victims.

Obviously, stopping a genocide before it actually happens is the most effective and least costly form of prevention.

Prevention Starts with Reducing Risk

Scholars have identified certain risk factors that make a society more likely to experience genocide. Countries with poor human rights records, for example, are typically at higher risk of genocide.

Poor economic conditions and a country's history of conflict are also factors that could contribute to large-scale violence against a group of people.

Migrants and refugees are people who are especially at risk of experiencing identity-based violence.

When more than 1 million Venezuelan refugees entered Colombia starting in 2015, for example, many risk factors were present. One risk factor is when a group has unequal access to basic resources and services.

The Colombian government saw this as a risk factor and responded. It introduced a new policy in February 2021 that gave temporary legal status to all refugees. This gave them access to public services, education and health care, immediately lowering the risk for large-scale violence in Colombia.

True Prevention Starts at Home

Every country in the world features some risk factors associated with genocide, including the United States.

But not every country in the world has the same level of risk.

In recent years, many countries have recognized the need to assess their own genocide risk factors. Some have fashioned specific government initiatives focused on genocide prevention. This work spans government departments and ministries to make sure governments keep genocide prevention in focus. Argentina, Mexico, Tanzania and Uganda are among the countries to undertake this kind of work.

The United States also has a national strategy focused on genocide prevention, though it does not look inward at this point —it is only concerned with atrocity prevention in other countries.

There are also several nongovernmental organizations that assist governments in prevention work, including the institute where I work.

Prevention Isn't Over When the Genocide Stops

There could be temptation to think that when mass killing stops, the work of prevention is finished. But one of the biggest genocide risk factors is if a society has already been involved with one. For example, the Holocaust happened only a couple decades after Germany perpetrated the genocide of Herero and Nama people in present-day Namibia.

For this reason, the work of prevention continues, even after a genocide is over.

This requires societies to deal with the risk factors that allowed genocide to take place, even as they rebuild.

For instance, after the 2007 elections in Kenya, massive inter-ethnic electoral violence broke out, killing over 1,000 people and displacing at least 350,000. The United Nations and the Kenyan government collaborated with nonprofits and local leaders to develop an early-warning network called the Uwiano Platform for Peace. This provides a hotline system where ordinary citizens can call or text if they hear hate speech or see violent acts. The information is then verified and, if it is credible, the central platform contacts local authorities to respond.

Following the implementation of Uwiano, no large-scale violence was reported after the 2010 and 2013 elections. Of course, Uwiano was not the only reason that Kenya avoided this violence. It took many international, national and local experts and others working together.

There is no single way to prevent genocide. What is clear, however, is that there are many different measures available that, together, can reduce the risk of genocide.

Periodical and Internet Sources Bibliography

The following articles have been selected to supplement the diverse views presented in this chapter.

Rayhan Asat, "When Do We Call Russia's Atrocities a Genocide?" *Lawfare*, May 25, 2022. https://www.lawfareblog.com/when-do-we-call-russias-atrocities-genocide.

Joseph R. Biden, Jr., "A Proclamation on Human Rights Day and Human Rights Week, 2021," The White House, December 9, 2021. https://www.whitehouse.gov/briefing-room/presidential-actions/2021/12/09/a-proclamation-on-human-rights-day-and-human-rights-week-2021/.

Kelley Currie, "Democracies Must Stop Playing Games with Myanmar's Representation at the United Nations," *Just Security*, October 21, 2022. https://www.justsecurity.org/83714/democracies-must-stop-playing-games-with-myanmars-representation-at-the-united-nations/.

Conor Finnegan, "Biden Calls Russia's Killing of Ukrainian Civilians a War Crime but Not Genocide," ABC News, April 4, 2022. https://abcnews.go.com/Politics/biden-calls-russias-killing-ukrainian-civilians-war-crime/story?id=83865128.

Mary Gerisch, "Health Care as a Human Right," American Bar Association, November 19, 2018. https://www.americanbar.org/groups/crsj/publications/human_rights_magazine_home/the-state-of-healthcare-in-the-united-states/health-care-as-a-human-right/.

Tom Gjelten, "Boundlessly Idealistic, Universal Declaration of Human Rights Is Still Resisted," NPR, December 10, 2018. https://www.npr.org/2018/12/10/675210421/its-human-rights-day-however-its-not-universally-accepted.

Philip Gourevitch, "Is It Time to Call Putin's War in Ukraine Genocide?" *New Yorker*, March 13, 2022. https://www.newyorker.com/news/daily-comment/is-it-time-to-call-putins-war-in-ukraine-genocide.

Kingsley Ighobor, "Genocide Happens When Democracy Is Absent," *Africa Renewal*, August 18, 2020. https://www.un.org/

africarenewal/magazine/august-2020/genocide-happens-when-democracy-absent.

Ryan W. Miller, “What is a War Crime? Ukraine Accuses Russia of Them, But What Exactly Constitutes a War Crime? *USA Today*, March 1, 2022. https://www.usatoday.com/story/news/world/2022/03/01/war-crimes-possible-punishment-if-found-guilty/6971469001/.

Anjli Parrin, “The Politics of Preventing Genocide,” the *New Humanitarian*, December 3, 2013. https://www.thenewhumanitarian.org/analysis/2013/12/03/politics-preventing-genocide.

For Further Discussion

Chapter 1

1. How do the viewpoints in this chapter define genocide? Are there any differences in these definitions?
2. From what you've read in the viewpoints in this chapter, do you think there is a meaningful difference between genocide and other crimes against humanity, such as ethnic cleansing? Explain your reasoning.
3. Based on the viewpoints in this chapter, what are some factors that caused genocides in the past? What causes them today? Provide examples from the viewpoints.

Chapter 2

1. According to the viewpoints in this chapter, how does racism play a role in facilitating acts of mass violence?
2. What are some of the instances of racially motivated mass violence that have occurred in U.S. history mentioned in this chapter? Do you believe any of them should be considered genocides? Explain your answer.
3. The viewpoint from the *Los Angeles Times* Editorial Board asserts that more should be done to atone for racism in the United States. Do you agree with their suggestions for how to do this? Why or why not? Do you have other ideas for how the U.S. government could atone for racism?

Chapter 3

1. Based on your understanding of genocide so far, do you believe that the Russia-Ukraine war is a genocide? Back up your argument with specifics from the viewpoints.
2. The viewpoint from the United Nations argues that no country is immune to the risk of genocide. Based on what you've learned about genocide, do you agree? Explain your reasoning.

3. What can individuals do to keep themselves and members of their communities from committing the practice of dehumanization, based on points made in these viewpoints?

Chapter 4

1. Multiple viewpoints in this chapter argue that democracy helps prevent genocide and other acts of mass violence. What are some of the reasons provided in these viewpoints? Do you agree? Why or why not?
2. What can individuals, schools, or local governments do to help prevent conflict and encourage trust in the government in order to enhance democracy? Back up your response with details from the viewpoints.
3. How can social media play a part in preventing genocide, based on the viewpoints in this chapter?

Organizations to Contact

The editors have compiled the following list of organizations concerned with the issues debated in this book. The descriptions are derived from materials provided by the organizations. All have publications or information available for interested readers. The list was compiled on the date of publication of the present volume; the information provided here may change. Be aware that many organizations take several weeks or longer to respond to inquiries, so allow as much time as possible.

Amnesty International

322 8th Avenue
New York, NY 10001
(212) 807-8400
website: www.amnesty.org/en/

Amnesty International is a global organization with over 10 million people actively engaged to protect human rights around the world. Learn all about protecting human rights, which is a step in the direction of ending violence and genocide. Amnesty International gives suggestions on how individuals can help in as little as a minute.

Auschwitz Institute for the Prevention of Genocide and Mass Atrocities (AIPG)

2 West 45th Street, Suite 1602
New York, NY 10036
(212) 575-2605
email: info@auschwitzinfo.org
website: www.auschwitzinstitute.org

The AIPG is a nonprofit organization that is working to build a world that prevents genocide and other mass atrocities. They are centered in Poland, the site of Auschwitz, one of the most infamous German concentration camps from the Holocaust. They have a wealth of information about genocide on their site. Of most interest is the section that profiles people around the world making a difference working against violence.

Commission on Security and Cooperation in Europe (CSCE)

234 Ford House Office Building
3rd and D Streets SW
Washington, DC, 20515
(202) 225-1901
email: INFO@CSCE.GOV
website: www.csce.gov

The CSCE is a U.S. governmental mission to promote human rights and security in 57 countries in Asia, Europe, and North America. Use the "by issue" tab to find information about genocide, war crimes, and crimes against humanity.

Genocide Watch

3351 N. Fairfax Drive, MS4D3
Arlington, VA 22201
(202) 643-1405
email: communications@genocidewatch.org
website: www.genocidewatch.com

Genocide Watch has a mission to predict, prevent, stop, and punish perpetrators of genocide and other forms of mass atrocities. Find up-to-date information about genocide and other mass violence and efforts to prevent these conflicts through articles, blogs, alerts, and social media.

Georgetown Institute for Women, Peace, and Security (GIWPS)

1412 36th Street, NW
Washington, DC 20057
(202) 525-1980
email: GIWPS@GEORGETOWN.EDU
website: https://giwps.georgetown.edu/

The GIWPS is an institute that recognizes that women are the key to sustainable peace and works to focus on the ability of women to promote global peace and prevent conflict. You can read articles on how the organization fulfills its mission on its website.

Modern Diplomacy

website: https://moderndiplomacy.eu/

Modern Diplomacy is an online news site that provides information about important world issues. Watch videos, read articles, and use the search function to find important news about genocide on the website.

National Endowment for Democracy (NED)

1201 Pennsylvania Ave., NW, Suite 1100
Washington, DC, 20004
(202) 378-9700
email: info@NED.org
website: www.ned.org

The NED is a private, nonprofit organization that is dedicated to strengthening democracy around the world, which can in turn lead to greater political stability and less violence. Read NED's blog for informative news.

United Nations (UN)

405 East 42nd Street
New York, NY 10017
(212) 963-4475
website: www.un.org/en/

The UN is an intergovernmental organization that seeks to promote peace, dignity, and equality on a healthy planet. Their site offers a wealth of information on issues of global importance. Use the search function to discover information directly related to the issue of genocide.

U.S. Department of State

Harry S. Truman Building
2201 C Street, NW
Washington, DC 20520
1 (888) 407-4747
website: www.state.gov

The U.S. Department of State is an executive department of the U.S. federal government that is responsible for the country's foreign policy and relations. They work to protect and promote U.S. security by shaping the international environment. Use the search function to find in-depth information about the issues surrounding genocide.

U.S. Holocaust Memorial Museum

100 Raoul Wallenberg Place, SW
Washington, DC 20024
(202) 488-0400
website: www.ushmm.org

The U.S. Holocaust Memorial Museum supports an online trove of information about the Holocaust and has a separate section all about confronting and preventing genocide. It also gives individuals ideas on how to take action.

Bibliography of Books

Mari Bolte. *Volodymyr Zelensky: Heroic Leader of Ukraine.* Minneapolis, MN: Lerner Publications, 2023.

Tamara L. Britton. *War in Ukraine.* Minneapolis, MN: Abdo Publishing, 2023.

James Bulgin. *The Holocaust.* London, UK: Imperial War Museum, 2021.

Jonathan Greenblatt. *It Could Happen Here: Why America is Tipping from Hate to the Unthinkable—and How We Can Stop It.* Boston, MA: Mariner Books, 2022.

David M. Haugen. *Were Native Americans the Victims of Genocide?* San Diego, CA: Reference Point Press, 2018.

Nicki Hitchcott. *Rwanda Genocide Stories: Fiction After 1994.* Liverpool, UK: Liverpool University Press, 2021.

Kristin Levine. *The Thing I'm Most Afraid Of.* New York, NY: G. P. Putnam's Sons, 2021.

Alexandra Lohse. *Prevail Until the Bitter End: Germans in the Waning Years of World War II.* Ithaca, NY: Cornell University Press, 2021.

Liam McDonald. *Indigenous America.* New York, NY: Penguin Workshop, 2022.

Jean Mendoza. *An Indigenous Peoples' History of the United States for Young People.* Boston, MA: Beacon Press, 2019.

Carla Mooney. *The Holocaust: Racism and Genocide in World War II.* White River Junction, VT: Nomad Press, 2017.

Rachel Morlock. *Rwanda* (Cultures of the World). 3rd ed. New York, NY: Cavendish Square, 2021.

Christine Poolos. *Myanmar* (Cultures of the World). 4th ed. New York, NY: Cavendish Square, 2022.

Sean R. Roberts. *The War on the Uyghurs: China's Internal Campaign Against a Muslim Minority.* Princeton, NJ: Princeton University Press, 2020.

Jessica Stern. *My War Criminal: Personal Encounters with an Architect of Genocide.* New York, NY: Ecco, 2020.

Christine Wilcox. *Understanding Violent Behavior.* San Diego, CA: Reference Point Press, 2018.

Index

N

P

R

S

T

U

V

W